More Weatherman Walks

More Weatherman Walks

Derek Brockway
and Julian Carey

Based on the BBC Wales
Radio and Television series Weatherman Walking

First impression: 2008
© BBC Wales and Y Lolfa Cyf., 2008

This book is subject to copyright and may not be reproduced by any means except for review purposes without the prior written consent of the publishers

The BBC Wales logo is a trade mark of the British Broadcasting Corporation and is used under licence. BBC Wales logo © BBC 1996

Published by Y Lolfa with the permission of the BBC

All maps reproduced by permission of Ordnance Survey on behalf of HMSO. © Crown copyright 2008. All rights reserved. Ordnance Survey Licence Number 100046541

Photographs by Julian Carey
Design: Y Lolfa

ISBN: 978 184771 058 1

Printed on acid-free and partly recycled paper and published and bound in Wales by
Y Lolfa Cyf., Talybont, Ceredigion SY24 5AP
e-mail ylolfa@ylolfa.com
website www.ylolfa.com
tel 01970 832 304
fax 832 782

Acknowledgements

I've really enjoyed doing another series of walks across Wales but I couldn't have done it without the help of so many kind and generous people. A big thanks to the guides for sharing their expertise and knowledge; to Julian Carey for his continuous enthusiasm and energy; the camera crew and production team for their patience and hard work, and to Christina Macaulay, our executive producer; to Clare Hudson and Martyn Ingram from BBC Wales for commissioning another series of the programme and to my editors Gail Morris Jones and Sali Collins, for allowing me to take time off from my forecasting duties; to Dafydd Saer of Y Lolfa; also to the Met Office for their support – and once again a huge thank you to Penny Arnold who first came up with the idea of a radio series called *Weatherman Walking* for BBC Radio Wales.

Pob hwyl!

Derek Brockway

Once again Derek has thanked all the right people for me already. We have a great crew of people who make the show happen and they make filming the series a holiday, not a job. Also thanks to all the Radio Wales teams who keep our *Weatherman Walking* on 657 and 882 Medium Wave (and 93–104 FM and Online and on Digital Satellite) when the telly show is off-air.

And thanks to Derek who is, as you'd expect, a lot of fun to work with. There's a reason he's such a favourite with people – he's genuine, down-to-earth, and what you see is what you get. Keep him topped up with chocolate biscuits and promise him a slap-up meal at the end of the day and he's very easy to work with. I look forward to pushing him up more mountains in the future.

Finally this book is for my family – my wife Nicky, and children Jack and Eve – thanks to them for letting me have a silly job on the telly and for being there when I come home at night. I love you all.

Julian Carey

Contents

Foreword

Hello, shw mae? Derek here with a second book of my favourite walks around Wales.

After the first book, lots of people wrote to us to say that they bought it and pledged to do every walk in the book – and it would be great if lots of people did that again. Basically *Weatherman Walking*, the radio and TV show, wants to be able to inspire you at home to want to get out and about and explore our wonderful country. The aim of the book is to get you walking through the year and to enjoy the different seasons. There are twelve walks in total, so you could do one a month. And let's face it, one walk a month isn't that much – we can all manage that.

I hope you like the book and the walks, which in my opinion are real gems. I've done them all and thoroughly enjoyed them. Remember, if I can do it – so can you!

Check the weather forecast before you set off (there's a bloke on the telly most nights on *Wales Today* who's more or less reliable!).

The main thing is to have fun and remember, whatever the weather, the outlook is bright and the sun is always shining above the clouds!

Pob lwc!

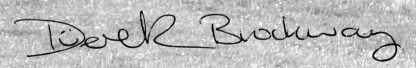

Introduction

Not many television programmes offer you the chance to walk in the footsteps of the presenter, to enjoy exactly the same experience as the 'experts' on the screen.

But *Weatherman Walking* exists to do just that.

We not only film some of the most exhilarating and breathtaking scenery in Wales but encourage people at home to pull on their walking gear and to get out and enjoy the great outdoors for themselves (we also encourage them to do this at the expense of watching more television – which on the face of it seems to be pretty misguided on our part!).

To do this we try and tap in to Derek's infectious enthusiasm for walking (and for his country) in the hope that it rubs off on the people watching at home and prods them in the direction of our glorious landscape. And if you have this book in your hands it's probably fair to say we might have succeeded.

Good! We want you to discover the fun of walking in Wales.

So we've designed the next twelve chapters to work as a year-long list of rambling suggestions to show you what Wales has to offer. And remember this only works out at one walk a month, leaving plenty of weekends available for you to do all the other things that complicate our free time – like shopping and DIY.

But before you pack your rucksack and head for the hills – a minor word of caution. Even though 99.9% of all country and hill walks pass off without a hitch or mishap, nobody wants to find themselves in the tiny minority that don't. Even the most inoffensive routes can cause someone to come a cropper and without getting all 'nanny state' over everything, it pays to exercise some caution. A little bit of planning before you set out – particularly if you're new to walking – will be time well spent.

Best foot forward

In the first *Weatherman Walking* book we devoted a whole chapter to walkers' safety, so it seems silly to do so again. But it is worth reiterating a few salient points.

Starting from your feet and working your way up, dress appropriately. Invest in a decent pair of boots, with good ankle support and proper protection. If you already have a trusty old pair of walking shoes lurking in a cupboard somewhere, check them before going out on the hills. Just like the tyres on your car, the tread on a pair of boots (even a good pair) will wear away. And just like the tyres on a car you'll need to replace them if they're worn down to a point where they can't grip as well as they used to.

As for the rest of your body, remember it's all about the weather – and being prepared for whatever Wales can throw at you. You need something waterproof and warm and, especially if you're heading up on to high ground. You also need to think about layers of clothing, so you can cool down or cosy up, depending on conditions.

To that end always take a small rucksack with you, to carry your extra kit. And try and pop some walking provisions in there too – even if it's just a bar of chocolate and a bottle of water – just to keep you 'fuelled up' on your hike. If you can squeeze in a torch, a whistle and a small first aid kit too then you won't go far wrong either. Take a mobile, but remember, chances are you won't get a signal when you need one, so always tell someone where you're going and when you should be back.

Finally pay attention to any weather warnings and check with local parks and guides before you set out, just in case there are any problems with the route. For example, when we were filming in Pontneddfechan for this latest series, the crew rendezvoused at the local Tourist Information Centre at the start of the walk. As we got ready, we noticed a stream of disappointed punters coming through the centre. They'd arrived hoping to attempt a particular waterfall path but had just found that it was closed due to a rock fall. Luckily for them there were plenty of other routes to choose from but it always pays to check conditions before you leave home.

A Cautionary Tale

If you need any encouragement to follow these rules and to think about safety, then the tragic story of Christopher Parrat might do the trick.

Mr Parrat, 32, was an experienced walker who died after he and his wife became confused in cloud while on Tryfan, one of the most challenging peaks in Snowdonia. The Oxfordshire couple had travelled to Gwynedd for a short holiday in June 2007 and after buying a guide book, a map and a compass, the pair decided to climb the mountain with their dog. The route they tried to follow had been recommended by their book as an easy path. But when they tried it, they found it to be more challenging than they expected.

When they finally got to the summit they found it covered in low cloud and turned back. On the way down, the conditions got wetter and the ground more slippery. They turned to the map to help navigate their descent but still lost the path. As the terrain became increasingly steep, Mr Parrat lost his grip and fell backwards from a ledge, landing 25 metres on the rock below. His wife called the emergency services before scrambling down to him and administering first aid. It took two hours for the Mountain Rescue team to reach them in the wet and misty conditions and by that time, there were no signs of life from the fallen walker.

Now Tryfan is a serious mountain and there is no easy way up or down it. But thousands of people do climb it without a hitch every year, and it's very popular with experienced walkers, some of whom brave the challenge of the 'leap of faith' – a terrifying jump across two tall columns of rock on the summit – something which would reduce most of us to jelly.

There's no suggestion that the couple were ill-prepared for their walk, that they failed to treat Tryfan with the required respect or that they were physically unable to cope with the mountain. But at the inquest, the coroner said she was concerned that the guide book had been the sole basis for the couple's decision to climb Tryfan. Experts at the inquest also questioned the detail on the map supplied by the guide, and suggestions that the route was relatively easy. Which brings us back to this book.

This is a book about walking in Wales, about the joy of the landscape and about what makes each of these walks special and interesting. It's not a guide book and shouldn't be used as such.

Over the next twelve chapters you'll find an equal number of maps which show the walks we covered for the most recent TV and radio series of *Weatherman Walking*. They are there to give you a rough idea of where the routes are, to provide a sense of direction and to help paint a picture of the broad sweep of the walk. And while all the walks are waymarked, we would encourage you to invest in a proper OS map before you set out, or, at the very least, to get additional information from the National Park or Local Authority responsible for the area. Because this book will not give you detailed directions or local maps. What it does give you is plenty of description as to what you'll find in these places. It's a companion piece to the television show, one that allows us to include information and stories which didn't make the final edited programme.

For instance while the Snowdon walk along the Watkin Path is onscreen for roughly 15 minutes, it took us two days to film the whole route. And if you intend to walk it, it will take you between four and five hours – maybe even a bit longer. Obviously then, there's a lot of detail about the routes and the places we visit which we are unable to include in the broadcast programmes. As such this book is a great opportunity for us to make sure that all those facts and figures that we've uncovered while making of the show never go to waste. But it's not a book to be slipped into your rucksack as your sole guide for a day's walking.

Take the first step

Finally, while some of the warnings and check lists might look scary, we really don't want to put you off walking, we just want to make sure that you do it safely.

After the first book was published we received lots of e-mails from people who said that they had been inspired to attempt all of the twelve walks featured in Weatherman walking. It would be great to think that the same happens this time. And even if you can't make all (or any) of the walks in this book, use it as a springboard to explore what's on your doorstep. You'll be doing yourself a big favour if you do. Not only will you benefit from the improved health and wellbeing that comes from regular walking, but a whole new world will be opened up to you. For example last Christmas, Derek and I went to Pontypool Park to record a festive walk up to the town's 'hilltop folly', for a series on Radio Wales. Now Derek's been to Pontypool on countless occasions and had even opened the leisure centre where the walk starts. But within five minutes of setting off he saw a completely different side to the town and, after half an hour, was rewarded with some fantastic views which easily matched those of more famous Welsh tourist hotspots.

The point is, he would never have tried a walk above Pontypool unless we had gone there to record a programme for Radio Wales. It just wouldn't have occurred to him. Yet unfortunately the same is true for the majority of people who live in that area. There are people who wake up every morning and see that Tower silhouetted on the hillside above, but who have never climbed the hill to experience it up close.

Torfaen Council, who maintain the park and the walks in the area, are actively promoting this and other routes in attempt to get their own residents and ratepayers to benefit from the beauty spots on their doorstep. They are not the only ones.

And while it's wonderful that Wales attracts so many visitors, we are very bad at getting our own people to appreciate and explore our gorgeous countryside. We are blessed with some of the best scenery in Britain. So enjoy it. Read this book, watch the television programme, tune in to the radio show and then get out there and see it, smell it, feel it and walk it for yourself. You won't regret it.

Julian Carey
Weatherman Walking Producer, BBC Wales

Pen-y-Fan

Near: Brecon

Ordnance Survey Grid Reference SO 986199

OS Explorer Map OL12

Derek says...

At 886 metres (2,907 ft) above sea-level, Pen-y-Fan is the highest peak in Britain south of the Snowdonia mountains. There are several ways up, but this route is one of the quickest and most popular, so it's advisable to arrive early.

The walk is easily accessible – being very close to the A470 – and if you are fit, you can be up and down in two or three hours. One of my favourite times of the year to come here is New Year's Day – it's a great way of clearing your head!

On a good day, there are wonderful views of Brecon and the surrounding countryside including the reservoirs, and if you are lucky, you may see a buzzard, merlin, peregrine falcon, red kite or sparrow hawk.

A word of warning, though: the weather can change quickly, so always come prepared and check the forecast before you set out. It can be mild and dry at the bottom but blowing a gale on the top, with rain and snow. Back at the car park, have a drink in the roadside café or visit the Brecon Beacons National Park Visitor Centre for lunch or tea – I often plump for the Welsh beef pie which is lush!

Pen-y-Fan, with its iconic flat-topped peak, is the highest point in southern Britain. The Brecon Beacons can appear rugged, barren and hostile, but if you look closely it is amazing what you can see. Watch out for kites and buzzards soaring overhead, listen for the skylarks singing their musical tune, smell the heather that covers whole areas in a deep purple blanket and touch the sandstone that formed the hills over 350 million years ago.

Central Brecon Beacons is a Site of Special Scientific Interest and in 2005 became the first area in Wales to be awarded Geopark status.

Make sure you are properly equipped for both the terrain and the changeable weather conditions that are not always as forecast (sorry, Derek!). Safety advice and weather forecasts can be found online at www.breconbeacons.org or by ringing our Visitor Centre on 01874 623366.

Jon Pimm
Brecon Beacons National Park Area Warden

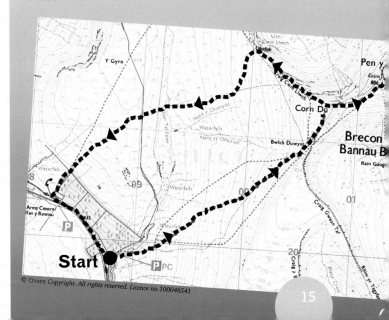

Start

Our first walk is one of the most popular in Wales – in fact one walkers' website nicknamed the main path here 'the motorway' because of the vast numbers who trawl up and down it.

Its iconic ridge and peak is recognised as the spiritual heart of the Brecon Beacons National Park and its steep, sharp climb also holds a special place amongst some of Britain's Armed Forces – although it's doubtful whether many of them remember it with much affection. It's also famous as a destination for walkers on Boxing Day and New Year's Day, when thousands of people head up to the main peaks. In fact the tradition for walking here over the Christmas holiday season has now evolved into a bizarre practice whereby small teams of people run the route at midnight on New Year's Eve – wearing head torches and carrying flashlights!

Nothing so exciting for us. When we visited Pen-y-Fan, we opted for an early Sunday morning climb and while it was still relatively busy, it wasn't crowded. So we still had a sense of having the place to ourselves and had time to dawdle and take the walk at our own pace. Which is just as well, because although the path is easy to follow, it's by no means an 'easy' walk.

This is, after all, the highest mountain in Southern Britain, standing 886 metres (2,907ft) above sea level, and is the highest peak south of Snowdon. It's also claimed a large number of casualties over the years. And if any further measure of its difficulty was needed, well Pen-y-Fan is also a training ground for some of the country's elite troops, including the SAS, who send would-be recruits here on a punishing run nicknamed 'the Fan Dance'.

Basically the soldiers are kitted out with a 35lb backpack and then split into two teams before being sent on a 24 km run. One team leaves from the Storey Arms centre and heads up to Pen-y-Fan, then down and around Cribyn before following the Roman Road until they reach Torpantau. They then turn around and head back the way they came. The other team starts from Torpantau and does the route in reverse. The time allowed for the run is 4 hours and 15 minutes.

This is not meant to be fun. And it isn't. So you'll be pleased to hear that our route is not quite so demanding nor is camouflage gear and an ability to kill with your bare hands a necessity of the walk either (although obviously Derek can do that – or so he tells us anyway).

Just like the SAS, you too could start the walk from the Storey Arms but we set out from the Pont ar Daf car park on the A470, which has the added attraction of a hot dog stand where you can grab a reviving cuppa on your way back down.

As walks go, Pen-y-Fan is all about exercise, achievement and breathtaking, beautiful views. Apart from a few ravens, there's little wildlife to speak of and the barren, bare hills offer little relief or colour. What you do get though is a taste of high-rise hill-walking, the cloud-busting 'top of the world' feel of a big mountain and an unparalleled view of the Beacons. Another bonus is that it's one of the easiest routes you'll follow with a clearly marked and well maintained path.

Although Pen-y-Fan is just 199 metres shorter than Snowdon, one of the attractions to novice walkers is that when your boots hit the tarmac at Pont ar Daf, you're already 400 metres above sea level when you begin walking. In contrast, when we walked Snowdon, we started at just a few metres above sea level – with all that height and climb ahead of us. So maybe it's not so surprising that Pen-y-Fan is so popular!

From the car park start, you cut through the conifers and cross a new footbridge, recently installed by National Park volunteers. It's a welcome addition to the trail, since before it was built, you started this route by fording the river over some stepping stones. One false move and the long climb ahead would be made even harder by a shoe full of freezing cold

water (or a 'soaker' as the locals would call it).

As you clear the tree line, you'll still hear the odd motorbike engine whine, the calling card of the speed merchants who use this stretch of the A470 as a race track. It's a temporary annoyance. All it takes is about ten minutes of steady walking to escape this last intrusion of the 21st century and from there on in, it's just you, the mountains and the sky above your head.

The path here is part of the long-distance Beacons Way route and benefits from being laid out in rough stone, with lots of drainage ditches giving you a soundtrack of babbling water as you get higher and higher. At this early point many walkers find themselves staring at the ground as the gradient begins to bite and they bend forward with gritted teeth and with ear cocked for the squeak of their knee caps! Rather than looking on this as a downside to the walk, use it as an opportunity to scan tough grasses for more appealing heathers and bilberries. Also those babbling streams are often frequented by dippers while above your head (if you can look up!) you should see buzzards or even a graceful red kite soaring above.

After ten minutes of climbing you should pause, take a deep breath and look around you. Do so and you'll be rewarded with some fantastic views. If you turn around on the path and look back across the valley, down to your left you'll see the Brecon reservoir (alongside the

A470) and to your right, you'll see Craig Cerrig Gleisiad, a National Nature reserve looked after by the Countryside Council for Wales. It was made a reserve back in 1958 and has a fascinating geology as well as lots of rare plants and trees, including the rare purple saxifrage, which normally only occurs in alpine conditions. It's also home to birds like the ring ouzel, the peregrine falcon and the wheatear and should you fancy it, footpaths are open to enable you to explore the reserve.

After thirty minutes of walking you should see the peak of Corn Du or 'the Black Horn' above you. It's a flat peak, a bit like a table top, and a lot of people mistake it for Pen-y-Fan. There isn't much between the two (Corn Du is the smaller peak at a mere 873 metres or 2,864 feet) and the slight difference allows it to mask the taller peak. In fact you don't catch sight of your destination until you're almost upon Bwlch Duwynt. Also known as 'the Windy gap' this is the saddle between Corn Du to the left and Duwynt to the right. It gets its name from the way the wind is funnelled through this space between the main ridges with ferocious intent.

To give you an idea of its power, the day we walked the path wasn't particularly windy, yet when we tried to record here we were nearly swept away and the wind noise made everything inaudible.

When we tried to record again about 100 yards above the gap, we watched as a walker below struggled to put his waterproof trousers on, the legs flying away from him like a flag as he battled to stay upright and get dressed at the same time!

Bwlch Duwynt is also the point where our path meets the main Pen-y-Fan circuit, a serious eight mile route that takes in both big peaks, plus Cribyn, Fan y Big and Graig Fan Ddu, via the old Gap road (thought to be Roman) and the Upper and Lower Neuadd reservoirs.

It's worth stopping here and dropping down below the rip and tear of the wind to soak up the first of the day's truly awe-inspiring views – after all this, is what you came here for.

Ten minutes of further hard walking gets you to the summit of Corn

Du. You pass a small black peat bog on the way before you hit the flat top summit with a burial cairn dating back to the Bronze Age. Once again it's all about the views here and at this western tip of the Pen-y-Fan horseshoe you look down on the village of Libanus to the north and down over the Usk Valley. Looking west on a clear day, you'll see Forest Fawr, and beyond that the Camarthen Fans stretching off into the distance. You also get the first sight of Pen-y-Fan's big draw: the awesome, dizzying drop from the top of the peak to the floor of Cwm Sere below. At over 1,000 feet straight down, it's not for the faint hearted, and that sheer fall is proof, if any was needed, of what a wild and potentially dangerous place this is.

Not that that stops the visitors. Over 100,000 people a year climb these peaks and from Corn Du, it's a gentle (well, a Welsh gentle) ten minute walk to the wide plateau of Pen-y-Fan – with spectacular views either side of the ridge along the way. There's no trig point here, so walkers tend to wander around, grabbing a little piece of the peak to themselves before dipping into their back pack rations and slowly letting the views overwhelm the senses.

The National Park office has photographs from the 1960s showing solitary walkers standing here in knee high grass, surveying the world below them. It's a different picture 50 years on from that. Human traffic and the wind and rain have taken that grass away and reduced the summit by a foot and a half of soil, leaving just the bare rock below. That's one of the downsides of Pen-y-Fan's popularity.

Chances are, though, at this point you won't be looking down at the ground beneath your feet – you'll be appreciating the view which you've walked and worked so hard for. On a clear day you'll see from the Black Mountains to the Preseli Hills, from Exmoor to Plynlimon and – if you're really lucky – you may even catch sight of Cader Idris in the distant north-west (but that would have to be an exceptionally clear day). If you find yourself with time here, then search out the small stone memorial dedicated to a young man who died after falling from the ridge here on the night of 17 March 1982. Trooper Waters was a 19-year-old commando

attached to the Royal Engineers and was on an SAS selection exercise when the tragedy struck. He was crossing the summit of Pen-y-Fan with another soldier, both men on their hands and knees due to the severe wind. When they realised they were getting closer to the cliff edge they stood up to get away from the edge and were both blown off the summit. Despite being injured, his colleague staggered down the mountain to get help, but it was too late. At the time of the accident, both men were within striking distance of the final checkpoint on the exercise and his story is another reminder of the respect walkers need to give Pen-y-Fan.

At this point, the ridge of Cribyn beckons and having climbed this far, the temptation is to keep on going, travelling along the trail at the top of the world, with just the ravens for company. But that's a longer walk for another day. Instead we headed back towards Corn Du and descended the ridge to take the downhill path towards the Storey Arms.

Steep at first, it soon eases out and should the fancy take you, you could take a slight detour on the route here and visit the Tommy Jones Obelisk. This is a memorial dedicated to a 5-year-old boy who in August 1900 got separated from his family while walking to his grandfather's farm at Cwm Llwch. The son of a Rhondda miner, he had been walking with his father when they met his cousin and grandfather on the hill. The two men stopped at an army camp and then told the two boys to walk on ahead of them up to the farm. It was dusk, and the story has it that Tommy began to get frightened in the gloom and shadows and was spooked by strange noises. He asked his cousin to walk him back to his father but he refused and told him to go back on his own.

He left the little boy and went on alone to the farm to tell everyone that Tommy and his Dad had arrived. That done he went back down to meet the party. As soon as he ran into them they realised that the little boy was missing and there followed a frantic search of the valley, with his family and the army combing the area, known locally as the Login.

For the next 29 days, teams of people searched for the boy. The London press picked up on the story and Tommy's fate became a national obsession. The Daily Mirror offered a £20 reward to anyone who could solve the mystery and a medium was prosecuted by magistrates after offering information on the boy. His body was eventually found on 2 September, but only after a particularly bizarre intervention. A Mrs Hamer of nearby Castle Madoc convinced her husband to take her to the mountain after being plagued by a dream she had, where the boy's body lay undisturbed in the long grass. She and her family had never visited the mountain but she felt sure she knew where he was.

They headed for Cwm Llwch and within a short time discovered the boy's remains. The obelisk marks the spot where they found him, just on the ridge above the Login, in the opposite direction to where Tommy was supposed to have headed. He had also climbed higher up the ridge than anyone would have expected a small boy to manage. Why he went the wrong way is a mystery to this day.

The memorial was paid for by voluntary subscription to a fund, started when the jurors at his inquest waived their fees. The £20 reward money was also donated to that fund. To this day, many walkers take time to visit the sad little spot and to pay their respects.

From the memorial you could also take a longer detour and visit the little lake of Cwm Llwch, a corrie lake left behind when the glacial ice receded from the north-facing cwms of the Beacons. It's a fine place for a picnic if you've anything left in your rucksack, but most people head straight down to the Storey Arms. It's a place named after a pub that, unfortunately for many of us who do the walk, was demolished back in 1924. The building that stands there now is a former youth hostel, which these days operates as an outdoor pursuits centre (there's a replacement hostel a few miles closer to Brecon).

From here you hit the main road and then it's a short downhill trek back to the Pont ar Daf car park. Granted this walk is no more than a straight up and down route to a bare headed mountain, but I can guarantee that after touching the sky above the Beacons you'll vow to return here again and again.

Very few walks can offer you a big mountain experience like this with such a relatively straightforward route. Similarly not many places will give you the choice of either mixing with the crowds for a really social walk or allowing you the space and freedom to find your own part of the mountain and claim your own piece of Pen-y-Fan.

As walks go, this is a keeper.

Newborough Beach

Near: Beaumaris, Anglesey

Ordnance Survey Grid Reference SH 426647

OS Explorer Map 262

Derek says...

Some say Anglesey is one of the most beautiful places in the world, and I can see why. This walk boasts a forest, wonderful beaches and lovely scenery. On a clear day the views towards Snowdonia and the Llŷn Peninsula are breathtaking.

The forest at Newborough is full of life and is home to red squirrels, bats and even a raven roost. The sand dunes are the largest in Wales, with a wide variety of wild flowers. They were formed in the 13th century when storms buried the area under a blanket of sand. Walking on the sand can be tricky; otherwise this walk is ideal for the whole family.

Before crossing over to Llanddwyn Island, check the tide times – and look out for the volcanic rocks sticking out of the sand, created when hot blobs of lava cooled rapidly as they were forced out of underwater volcanoes, creating bumpy pillow-like shapes.

Llanddwyn Island is a special place, with beautiful coves and ideal beaches for swimming. It is also the home of the patron saint of Welsh lovers, Dwynwen, and is the perfect location for a romantic stroll. The Isle of Anglesey Walking Festival in June is a good way of discovering this superb walk and others along the coastal footpath.

This walks takes you into one of the finest and most spectacular sand dune systems in Europe, and has something for everyone. In the summer months the dunes are awash with colourful plants and butterflies, whilst the associated estuaries and salt marshes are a paradise for bird watchers year round. If you are lucky you may also see a red squirrel in the neighbouring coniferous plantation.

Why not take a paddle or just relax on some of the finest beaches in Wales as part of your walk? Or if it's history you're after, there's plenty on the tranquil and romantic island of Llanddwyn – home of Welsh patron saint of lovers, St Dwynwen. Legend has it that all lovers who venture here will be happy for the remainder of their days. The pilots' cottages, lifeboat houses and lighthouse are a reminder of the island's maritime past.

At all times please be aware of tides.

Will Sandison

25

Every summer, Anglesey holds a nine-day walking festival and plays host to the hordes of visitors who flood in to the island to sample its many and varied delights. But when it comes to this walk, maybe you should schedule your visit to Ynys Môn just a little bit earlier in the year – say 25 January or even 14 February.

Why? Well this route is arguably the most romantic walk in Wales: a hand-in-hand stroll of just under six miles around Llanddwyn Island, the home of St Dwynwen, the Welsh patron saint of love and friendship. But that's not to say that this walk is just for star-crossed lovers and wistful romantics. It's an incredibly rich walk, both in terms of history and heritage as well as wildlife. And while it may be physically undemanding, the walk takes you through protected nature reserves, four different eco-systems and some truly spectacular scenery.

Quite simply it's one of the most beautiful places in Wales, 365 days of the year.

In fact, catch this magical spot on the right day and you'll be hard-pressed to find a better stretch of sand and sea anywhere in the world. The beach here stretches for three glorious miles and in the winter months is often totally deserted, allowing you to lie back in the dunes and take in the awe-inspiring backdrop of the Snowdonia mountain range, stretching from the Menai Strait down to Bardsey Island.

So where do we start? Well, the beach, sand dunes and coastal pine forest that make up this fascinating walk all lie on the outskirts of the town of Newborough, in the south west corner of the island. The town was founded in the late 1200s when the inhabitants of Llan-faes were evicted to make way for Beaumaris Castle (making it a *new borough*, hence the name). Previously the area had housed one of the ancient courts of the Welsh princes, the great hall of Llys Rhosyr, the remains of which lie about two miles above the beach, just to the west of the local parish church of Saint Peter's. If you're doing the walk it's worth a detour to take a look. Recently excavated, it is the only surviving site of its kind in North Wales, and while it's hardly the most awe-inspiring set of ruins, you can appreciate the scale of the old palace with the remains of the court's perimeter wall, main hall and the prince's chambers all clearly visible.

Sculptures representing marram grass in the Llyn Rhos Ddu car park in Penlon.

Around the time of Newborough's creation the sand began to have a major impact on the land here. As the people forced into the area began to farm the shallow and largely infertile soil at Newborough, they quickly eroded the ground, creating 'dust bowl' conditions. Soon the destabilised dune system began to blow inward and in 1330 a great storm caused over 200 acres of land here to be covered in sand. Storms continued to have a similarly disastrous effect throughout the Middle Ages, and in Elizabethan times, laws were passed to stop the local marram grass being harmed, as the plant's root system was one of the few things still holding the dunes

27

together. It's apt, then, that the start of the walk is all about the dunes and the marram grass.

The Llyn Rhos Ddu car park in Penlon is one of the easiest you'll ever find, thanks to three extraordinary bright yellow metal sculptures which stand over 20 feet tall and sit smack in the middle of it. They are artistic interpretations of Gafrod – the local word for bunches of marram grass, stacked on end and tied at the top. The sculpture is a memorial to the local marram-weaving industry which was exclusive to this area right up until the 1930s. The grass was important to the environment as well as to the working lives of the people here. While the roots of the plant were left to anchor the sand, the leaves were woven and used to make brooms, baskets, nets, ropes and matting. Marram products were exported all over Britain – a vibrant local trade until the turn of the last century (in fact the very last marram mats were woven in 1948 and donated to the Welsh Folk Museum at St Fagans).

The grass itself grows just beyond the warren, which begins the other side of car park. The warren, the beach, the island of Llanddwyn and the salt marshes are all managed as a National Nature Reserve by the Countryside Council for Wales (as is Newborough Forest at the end of the walk).

As its name suggests it was once home to thousands of rabbits who provided another living for the people of the town. However the warren was seriously depleted thanks to forestry plantation after the Second World War, while the remaining rabbit population was decimated by the first myxomatosis outbreak in 1954.

The warren and dune system are great for walkers, and dozens of trails criss-cross the up and down bounce of the landscape here, teasing you with glimpses of the Menai Straits, Caernarvon and the mountain ranges beyond. They are also home to a host of plants and wildlife. Dune pansies, sea spurge and sand cat's-tail grow alongside the marram grass while in the hollows of the dune slacks you'll find creeping willow and a variety of orchids including the marsh orchid along with butterwort, grass of Parnassus and yellow bird's-nest.

If you're lucky you might see toads or lizards creeping through the colourful undergrowth but you're more likely to see birds like curlews, lapwings, meadow pipits, skylarks and oystercatchers. Obviously you'll still see the odd rabbit too, although they're nowhere near as abundant as they used to be (at their height the population was supplying local rabbit catchers with over 100,000 animals a year).

From the Warren, you move into the second of the four distinct habitats on this walk, the salt marshes of Traeth Melynog. Time your visit with the tides and you'll see this otherworldly landscape at its best, exposed and slickly glistening like a long flat muddy runway to the Straits beyond it.

In fact the landing strip analogy is apt, as the marsh provides not

so much a drive-through fast food outlet but a fly-in free-for-all for migrating birds. It's one of the most important feeding grounds for (mostly Scandinavian) migrating birds stopping in Britain on their way to Africa. Visiting species include redshank, widgin, teale, grey leg geese, shellducks, ringed plovers and pintails. You'll also see curlews, mute swans, sedge warblers, reed warblers and occasionally (in the winter months) marsh and hen harriers.

No wonder then that the area was a happy hunting ground for the acclaimed wildlife artist Charles F Tunnicliffe who moved here in 1947. The island now houses a permanent exhibition of his work (which was purchased after his death in 1979) at Oriel Ynys Môn.

The marsh isn't the best place for walkers, but tread carefully and stick to the dune side of the divide, and you'll be rewarded with some fantastic views of Caernarvon Castle and the mountains beyond.

You can also see Abermenai Point, mentioned in the Mabinogion as the place where a royal fleet of thirteen ships left for Ireland following the marriage of Branwen to the Irish King Matholwch. It was also an important harbour linking the royal palace with the mainland as well as the site of an ancient ferry route to Ireland. The Romans once eyed it as a potential landing point for an invasion of Anglesey and many years later, it was the place where Prince Llywelyn anchored his fleet (the only time when Wales was able to boast its own navy!).

Cutting across the dunes there's plenty of opportunity to enjoy the flora and fauna before you finally hit that long, long beach. It can attract kite surfers and kite buggy riders, but if the thrill seekers aren't around this is about as pleasant a beach walk as you'll get. It attracts over 100,000 visitors a year but it's such a vast stretch of sand that it easily absorbs those numbers, and outside of the summer you'll more or less have it to yourself.

Most visitors to Newborough drive straight to the beach through the forestry (there is an automated toll road that gives you access to the car park and toilet facilities – you'll need £2 to get you through the barrier and then you're in). But whether you walk here or drive in, it's a peach of a beach, a natural, unspoilt, soft and sandy blanket with amazing views.

And while the skyline is dominated by the jagged shapes of Snowdonia, the blue silhouettes of Yr Eifl (the Rivals) and the smaller hills of Llŷn, you may be lucky to spot the remains of an old shipwreck if you lower your line of sight. Known locally as Y Llong Roegaidd (the Greek Ship), it breaks the water at low tide and is all that remains of a brig called the Athena that sank in 1852 en route to Liverpool.

After a mile and a half of relaxed walking you can shake the sand from your shoes and head on to the island.

Now obviously you don't just walk onto an island – Llanddwyn is connected to the mainland by a causeway and is only cut off from the land by high tides. The neck of rock that connects the two pieces of land attracts a fair share of visitors too – although they tend to be hardcore geologists. The reason? Well, it's made up of pillow lava which was thrown up by a volcanic eruption over 570 million years ago. During the Cambrian period, much of Wales was under water, covered by the ancient Iapetus Ocean. The only break in the liquid monotony came from lava spewed up from submerged volcanoes which then cooled into folds of molten rock. It's the remains of this activity that you walk over to get to Llanddwyn.

Once you've crossed, you are rewarded with another set of stunning views, this time looking back to Newborough beach, the pine forest and the hidden bay of Malltraeth Sands. It looks like an idealised version of

the New England coastline – it certainly doesn't look like Wales – and it's a dramatic introduction to this special little island which has an atmosphere all of its own.

It takes five minutes to cross onto the peninsula but you can feel centuries fall away with each step onto the island proper. For such a small island there is much to make you wander and idle, with a lighthouse, a ruined church, a row of pilots' cottages and the daredevil swoops of seabirds all vying for your attention.

Of course the main attraction is Dwynwen, the lovelorn saint who made the island her home. During the making of the programme we heard at least four different versions of the story of Dwynwen and a quick search of the internet reveals many more variations on the theme. This is the version

we're sticking to however (even though it's slightly different from that of Will, our television guide).

Dwynwen lived during the fifth century and was one of King Brychan Brycheiniog's 24 daughters. She fell in love with a man named Maelon Dafodrill but unfortunately her father had already arranged for her to marry someone else.

When Maelon discovered her father's plans, he flew into a rage and took out his anger on Dwynwen, raping the poor girl and then leaving her. The grief-stricken princess fled to the woods where she fell down on her knees and begged God to make her forget Maelon, before falling into an exhausted sleep. It was then that she was visited by an angel who first froze Maelon inside a block of ice and then offered Dwynwen a sweet potion which would erase all memory of her brutal former lover. God then gave the girl three wishes. She used the first to thaw out Maelon and release him, the second to fix it so that she never married and the third, to ask God to fulfil the hopes and dreams of all true lovers. In return she then promised to devote herself to God's service.

In other versions of the story, one of the wishes was used to keep Dwynwen on the island for the rest of her life. And if you were going to banish yourself to one particular place in Wales, you could do a lot worse than Llanddwyn.

There are a number of small bays and beaches where you can tumble down onto the sand and search for shells or watch the sea birds, like the stiff black cormorants who patrol the rocks beneath the lighthouse.

You can also visit the remains of Eglwyseg Dwynwen, the 16th century church dedicated to Dwynwen, allegedly built on the site of her original church, which she established over 1,100 years earlier. The dilapidated state of the building is said to be due to the removal of stone and timbers in the early 19th century for boat building and to provide materials for a navigation beacon.

Just beyond the ruins are Tai Peilot, a row of cottages built around 1826

which housed the pilots who guided the ships down the Menai Strait. These days they have been restored and are maintained in a traditional style and one of them houses a permanent exhibition to the island's maritime heritage. The pilots also manned the local lifeboat and the cannon which was used to call the crew to action is displayed outside the cottages (the lifeboat service was disbanded here back in 1903. In their time they saved over 100 people).

There are also two crosses on the island: a Celtic-style cross inscribed with Dwynwen's name and the date of her death (25 January 465); and a tall traditional cross overlooking the church and lighthouse, erected in Victorian times.

As for the lighthouse, it's the second beacon built on the island (the first was Tŵr Bach, established at the tip of the island in 1800) and was designed in the style of the many windmills that used to be dotted all over Anglesey.

Built in 1845, Tŵr Mawr (the big tower), was the focal point of a Hollywood film set back in 2004, when the Demi Moore movie *Halflight* was shot on Llanddwyn island. The lighthouse isn't open to the public but

you can walk up to the tower and around it. It makes for a great place to soak up the view and keep a look out for seals and sea birds. From here you then head back onto the mainland and cut through the peaceful, pine-columned avenues of Newborough Forest. It's the fourth and final habitat that you wander through (after the dunes, salt marsh and warren) and is another amazing contrast in this rich and varied walk.

It's also a place where – if you're really lucky – you might spot a rare red squirrel, as Newborough has the second largest population in Wales (and is the only place in the Principality where they don't have to compete with the greys that have driven them out of so many other habitats).

Walking through the scented Corsican pines, you catch glimpses of the glory of Llanddwyn beyond the tree line, while at your feet, wildflowers like marsh and bee orchids, wintergreen and bright blue viper's bugloss, distract and delight. It's a designated Site of Special Scientific Interest and birdwatchers might be tempted to dwell awhile to try and spot the crossbills and goldfinches who make their home here.

There are a number of criss-crossing trails and footpaths to follow in the forest if you have the time, as well as the remains of a medieval house (called the Hendai) which was abandoned after being covered by sand, during the same storms that created the dune system. In fact the forest was planted on former sand warrens and you can sometimes spot the shape and twist of the old dune system beneath the trees.

Newborough Forest is a commercial plantation and a relatively new addition to the landscape, having been planted between 1948 and 1965. Currently there is a debate as to whether or not large parts of the forest should be felled and the original land restored. Whatever the merits of that argument, its cool shadows make for a relaxing end to what really is a special and unique Welsh walk.

Dylife

Near: Machynlleth, Powys

Ordnance Survey Grid Reference SH 862941

OS Explorer Map 215

Derek says...

There's plenty to see on this walk, including a nature reserve, old mines and a mini 'Grand Canyon'. This area also has lots of history and a few gruesome stories.

On a clear day, you can see for miles: look out for Cadair Idris and Snowdon from the Wynford Vaughan Thomas Memorial. The landscape can be wild and desolate but also beautiful, with green rolling hills and farmland.

The walk passes through old mining country and some of the mines have collapsed, so take care and stick to the path. However, it is worth taking a small diversion to see Dyfrgwm Gorge, which is like something out of a Wild West cowboy movie! Two streams flow through the gorge: the Nant Goch (red stream) which gets its colour from the copper in the area, and the Nant Ddu (black stream) which gets its colour from peat.

At the Glaslyn Nature Reserve you may see birds of prey including red kite, merlin and peregrine. At the end of the walk, stop for a drink in the Star Inn, Dylife, which used to be a drovers' pub and dates back to the 17th century.

This section of Glyndŵr's Way has always been my favourite because of the contrast between the derelict remnants of long-forgotten industry at Dylife and the peace and tranquillity of the lake at Glaslyn. There's also a breathtaking transition from the remote and desolate beauty of the plateau to the stunning views westwards from Foel Fadian. From here (on a clear day!) one can see the rich, rolling green landscape of the Dulas and Dyfi valleys stretching down towards the sea, with a memorable backdrop of the Tarren hills and Cadair Idris.

Maybe I'm biased as this area links the Dyfi Valley – where I grew up – with the Llawryglyn and Trefeglwys areas north of Llanidloes where most of my family originally came from, but I consider myself very fortunate to live and work with such an incredible contrast of beautiful and tranquil landscapes right on my doorstep.

Rab Jones
Head Warden, Countryside Services, Powys County Council

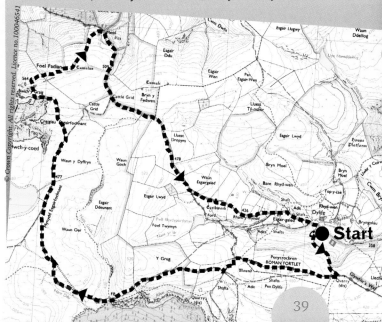

Start

Where in Wales would you go for a March walk? Given that the first of the month is the day of our national saint and a cause for celebration across the land, a March walk should have a suitably Welsh theme.

With a walk around St David's already recommended in our first book, we decided to target a section of Glyndŵr's Way, the 135-mile route named after the country's greatest hero.

The whole trail takes about nine days (on average) to complete and runs from Knighton, on the English border, in a loop through mid-Wales until it finishes alongside the Montgomeryshire Canal in Welshpool. The route follows various significant battle sites associated with the 15th century folk hero, who led a Welsh uprising and established a Welsh Parliament in the former capital of Machynlleth back in 1404.

Glyndŵr's Way was granted National Trail status back in the year 2000 and the section we've chosen is part of a circular walk that centres on the former lead mining village of Dylife. Not that there's much there these days. In fact this route is a real trip back through time, rich with stories of lost Roman roads, gruesome murders and a long gone industrial past.

It starts in a gravel-covered car park below the Star Inn, one of the few complete buildings in the landscape and overlooking what appears to be an

Your constant travelling companions – wherever you walk in Wales.

abandoned quarry site. Granted, this makes for an inauspicious beginning but you'll immediately find a good reason to choose this as a walk – particularly for inexperienced ramblers. For a start, no other walk we've yet come across gets you high as quickly as this. Let me explain. Just ten minutes of trudging up the one farm track that leads away from this scruffy car park and you are rewarded with some real, top of the world, wide-open spaces. It's the kind of terrain and view that ought to take an hour's worth of hard walking to achieve and yet here it's a fairly instant reward.

There are incredible far reaching views across the Hafren forest to the south, the Berwyn range to the north east, as well as glimpses of Plynlimon and Cadair Idris. In fact if you just did the Roman Road path for a mile and back across Pen-y-Crocbren, then you'd leave Dylife feeling totally de-stressed, energised by the sharp clean air and with your eyeballs singing from the sight of those hills rolling away before you.

Stand still here and you'll feel like a little human island in the middle of a vast, lush green ocean with nothing but blue sky above you, and the road a distant hum in the background. And that's just the start of this walk. The whole route delivers some unique landscapes, a taste of a lost Wales, countryside that changes in colour and form at the brow of every hill and an end view that Wynford Vaughan Thomas once claimed was the best in the whole country.

So forget that bleak, grey car park and instead pack a healthy imagination and an open mind alongside your waterproofs. Because with this walk, you have to dig a little (metaphorically speaking) below the surface of the landscape. Take that uninspiring car park for instance. Just below the pub is a ruined churchyard and if you have the time, take a quick look inside at the haphazard gravestones and get a sense of the people who used to live here.

They were people whose lives were bound to mining. Some historians believe mining for lead started here back in Roman times and a detailed history of the industry can be traced back to the 1600s. However, the boom time for the village was the 1800s when the operation here was the biggest

in Europe. In 1851 the largest water wheel in mainland Britain was built and operated at Dylife, a wooden monster which measured 63 feet in diameter by three and a half feet in breadth. It was worked at the site for over 50 years non-stop, its job being to pump and wind from the Llechwedd Du engine shaft.

It survived here until the early 1900s when it was dismantled and sent to Canada following the mine's closure. Once operations ceased it wasn't just the machinery that left the community. With no work, the people soon left too, many for the mines in South Wales. However as the cemetery demonstrates, they may have had to live in towns like Merthyr and Aberdare but they wanted to be buried in their home village of Dylife. Not that there is much of that village left now. Many of the buildings that sprang up around the mining industry were torn down once the shafts were closed, the stone and slate cannibalised for new homes and work places. So within a hundred years the area has been returned to how it was before mining started, with a few scattered farmhouses providing the only signs of human habitation in the landscape.

There are some souvenirs of Dylife's mining past though – and quite deadly ones at that. As you leave the car park and head onto the hills above, be careful not to stray too far from the path because the land here is dotted with old shafts. Some are fenced off but not all: some lie hidden, unknown even to the countryside wardens and the farmers who walk the hills every day. Fall into one of these black holes and your walking days are over.

The road soon turns into a sheep track once you get through a series of farm gates and it's worth remembering that before the road down the valley through Dylife was built, this was the main road between Llanidloes and Machynlleth. Locally it's known as a Roman road, but while it runs alongside the remains of a garrison hut that dates back to Roman times, it's not a Roman road as you might think of one. It's probable that this rough mountain track had been in use long before any centurion stumbled across it.

The garrison hut is a large square depression in the ground to the left of the track, about ten minutes walk from the farm gates. It's not much to look at and in truth at this point of the walk you'll still be marvelling at the wonderful 360-degree view of Montgomeryshire. It's a view that on a clear day is hard to beat. It's also one that allows you to clock the four huge wind farms that surround the skyline – Bryn Titli in Radnorshire, as well as those of Llandinam, Carno and Cemmaes in Montgomeryshire.

Not that the sound of these giants carries far enough to disturb your walk here. If you hear anything at all it will be the bleat of sheep that scatter over the surrounding green hills. And while the windmills on the horizon are not that dominant, it hasn't stopped some people labelling this stretch of Glyndŵr's Way the Turbine Trail!

Once you pass the Roman remains, look out for another smaller square-shaped hump just below them. This is the bizarrely named 'Gibbet Garden'.

It's one of the more grisly landmarks on the old highway and a

Look out below! One of the fenced-off fissures that dot the landscape – behind the wire is an exposed mine shaft that you really don't want to investigate.

place linked with a notorious Welsh murder. In 1719 a blacksmith from Cardiganshire called John Jones (or Sion y Gof as he's also known) left home in search of work in the booming mining town of Dylife. He left a wife and two children behind and soon found employment – and a new woman, a maid from nearby Llwyn y Gog. After a few months had passed with no word from John, his wife set out with the children in tow to track him down. She found him but he managed to hide his secret life from his family while they stayed with him for a short while. Satisfied that her husband was safe, well and keeping on the straight and narrow, his wife decided to return to her home with the children. John accompanied his family over the first part of the journey but on the lonely mountain road through Pen-y-Crocbren, he attacked them, throwing them down a disused mine shaft. He reasoned that friends and family in Cardiganshire would believe them settled in Dylife, while everyone in Dylife would assume they had gone back to their home village.

It was a simple plan and he might have got away with the triple murder had it not been for mine manager Colonel Ward. It was he who decided to open up some of the old shafts and reclaim the timbers from them. He sent three men into the closed sections of the mine and when they entered the tunnels they found the gruesome remains of the Jones family. The murderer was soon caught and in 1720 he was tried, found guilty and sentenced to death.

At this time, murderers would be left in gibbets near the roadside to deter others from committing similarly evil acts. And in a bizarre twist, as the town's only blacksmith, Sion y Gof had to make his own gibbet before he was hanged. His remains were left at this spot, the Gibbet Garden, not far from where the murders were committed.

For many years, people had speculated as to how much of this tale belonged to folklore and legend. Then in 1938 a local historian and former miner Will Richards set out with a friend, intent on putting the story to the test. After digging at the mound with a shovel, Will unearthed a human skull caught inside a rusted mask of iron attached to a rotting gibbet.

Sion y Gof, it seems, had never left the scene of the crime. The remains were excavated and the gibbet now rests in St Fagans Folk Museum.

Leaving Pen y Crocbren, you head straight for the edge of the hill in front of you, where the land begins to fall away into a gorge straight out of a Wild West movie. At this point you stray off Glyndŵr's Way but you're only dropping down about twenty yards below it to the edge of the hill and it's easy enough to get back on track. It's well worth taking the diversion as you get a great view of Castle Rock, the big stone buttress that dominates the gorge. This was another mining site and all around there's evidence of shafts, altered watercourses and leats.

Try and avoid the temptation to scramble down to the riverbed though. The way down is over a slippery sea of shale, which sucks you up to the ankles and moves like a conveyor belt under your feet, dragging you down and sending you sliding sideways. Not recommended. With the pine forests above the gorge and the worn rock at the sides of the river this does seem like a scene from an American Western, the hills made for horse riding and the abandoned mines giving it a forgotten frontier town feel. It is certainly unlike any other trail we've ever filmed in Wales.

Back on the main path you'll head away from the gorge, over a small wooden bridge into a collection of sheepfolds built alongside the remains of an old water wheel and former mine buildings. These are shearing pens and as such, not in use for most of the year.

As you walk out from the farm keep your eyes peeled at the side of the road for a small stone memorial. This is dedicated to Maurice Griffiths, the local farmer who owned the land and worked here, and who requested that his ashes were scattered on the hill when he died.

From here up until the lake of Glaslyn the scenery can be a bit bleak with just the sheep for company and the odd abandoned mine building to break up the view. And while the bare heath and moorland might not be everyone's cup of tea, it can be a deeply affecting landscape. If nothing else it acts as a contrast to the lush green farmland which is such a treat at the end of the walk.

In the middle of this dour scrub, Glaslyn looks like an oasis but it's not the most welcoming of watering holes. Such is the low nutrient level of the lake, nothing lives in it bar a specially adapted strain of pondweed, called quillwort.

However there is plenty of life around Glaslyn. At 540 acres it's the biggest nature reserve currently managed by the Montgomeryshire Wildlife Trust, with the flat plateau a home to wheatears, golden plovers, ring ouzels, meadow pipits and red grouse. The mix of heathers, bilberry and crowberry provide cover and food for the grouse as well as for other birds like skylarks. Diving ducks such as the goldeneye are winter visitors to the lake while the area is also a happy hunting ground for birds of prey, like kites and merlins.

There is a circular walk around the lake and a viewing point near the water's edge but probably the most amazing thing about this place is the steep ravine at the far side of Glaslyn where the ground drops away sharply to the Afon Dulas below.

From here you head up to Foel Fadian and the trig point at the top of the mountain. You have now left Glyndŵr's Way and begin a slow circular route back to Dylife. This part of the walk gives the best view of the lake and that steep drop down the ravine – which looks scarier and scarier the higher up you climb. It's a steep pull up to the trig point and in misty conditions (like the ones we filmed in) it's easy to lose your way here.

On a clear day though, that thigh burn of a climb is rewarded with a magnificent view across Montgomeryshire. In total contrast to the bog and moorland you've just been traversing, the land stretches out below you in a glorious patchwork quilt of luscious green farmland, dark woodland and purple-headed mountains, which roll down to the sea in the west.

As well as fantastic views of Cadair Idris and the Snowdonia range, to the west you'll see the sea and the glorious Dyfi estuary; to the south, mid Wales, Plynlimon, Ceredigion and Radnorshire. On a good day, the Aran and Berwyn ranges can be seen stretching away north eastwards towards the English border.

The trig point gives a much better view then the Memorial platform which lies about half a mile below it, next to the road. This is often celebrated as the best view in Wales – indeed that was the opinion of the man to whom the memorial is dedicated, Wynford Vaughan Thomas. The famous broadcaster, journalist and author is portrayed on the slate toposcope pointing towards Snowdon, which you might be able to see from here on an exceptionally clear day.

The memorial also handily reels off the names of all the mountains and ranges on the horizon and, as it sits just twenty yards from the roadside, it means that even non-walkers can get a taste of this wonderful landscape. The trig point still beats it though!

From the memorial you head for the road and follow it back to the Star Inn and our starting point. It's about a mile and half of tarmac with not much to recommend it but at this point you've already feasted on some of the finest scenery in mid Wales. And the great thing about this route for non-walkers is that you can get to two of the main viewpoints from the road. You can even drive to Glaslyn, although be warned the road can be a bit worn and bumpy and does ask questions of even the most forgiving suspension. If you still want more views to die for, head back down the road away from Machynlleth and stop off for two classic road side panoramas.

The first is the Dylife Gorge, a v-shaped ravine that stretches for miles, while the second is the Clywedog Reservoir, which comes with its own 'pull-in-and-park-up' picnic spot. But if you decide to do the short hand version of this walk and scoot from point to point by car, remember one thing: the scenery might look great through the windscreen, but it's a lot better when you walk it.

Pontneddfechan

Near: Merthyr Tudful

Ordnance Survey Grid Reference SN 903076

OS Explorer Map OL12

Derek says…

This walk is a real treat – full of stunning scenery, industrial history and deep woodland gorges. It's also great if you like geology, as there are limestone pavements, old silica mines, tumbling waterfalls and a large cave.

We filmed this walk in summer 2007 which turned out to be the wettest in Wales since 1912! The trees did provide some cover from the rain but we still got soaked – at one point I could feel the water running down the back of my neck!

In July the rivers would normally be a trickle, but on this occasion they were very swollen. Mind you, the extra rainfall did boost the waterfalls, including Sgwd Gwladus, or 'Lady Falls'. The sound of the water hitting the river below was deafening, so bring your earplugs!

Take care in wet weather because it can get slippery. There have been fatalities, so wear footwear with good soles and keep an eye on children. The cave at Porth yr Ogof is amazing, but don't venture inside without proper caving equipment and supervision. There are other attractions to see along the way too, such as Dinas Rock – which is the best cliff in South Wales for rock climbing – plus a wide variety of bird and plant life, including rare orchids.

Pontneddfechan was once a scene of great industrial activity and innovation. Today, visitors are drawn here to explore the fascinating relics of its industrial past and access the Waterfalls Area – one of the most popular and beautiful parts of Brecon Beacons National Park. Geology, natural history and clean, fast-flowing rivers have all combined to create a very special and magical place.

Beginning in the late 18th century, mines exploited Dinas silica rock or quartzite, providing the material for manufacturing firebricks which were used to line furnaces. The firebricks were exported worldwide, contributing significantly to South Wales' role as a major player in the Industrial Revolution. The mines have been abandoned since 1964, so the disused tree-lined tramways – a legacy of the area's industrial exploitation – now provide easy access into this wild and beautiful countryside.

Tony Ramsay

Scientific Director,
Brecon Beacons
Fforest Fawr
Geopark

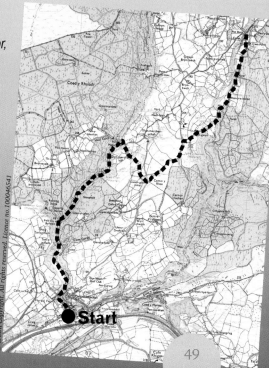

Start

49

If we all agree that Wales has more than its fair share of April showers then where should we go to make the most of our naturally occurring downpours? Well, how about a walk through wet and wild waterfall country? Because this is one walk where the rain adds something to the spectacle and at least the heavily-wooded gorges can provide some shelter on a squally day.

So the Beacons makes its second appearance in the book by virtue of this route around Coed y Rhaeadr, which kicks off from the new Waterfalls Centre in Pontneddfechan (just above Glyneath). The Waterfall Area is one of the most popular and beautiful parts of the National Park. It's where the rivers Mellte, Hepste and Nedd Fechan (all tributaries of the River Neath) congregate and wind their way through a landscape sculpted out of hard sandstone and soft black shale. Gradually those rivers have worn away at the shale, leaving the water to plunge and pour over the remaining sandstone ledges, in a series of dramatic falls.

There are a number of paths here, maintained by the National Park and the Forestry Commission, which allow you to explore the humid shade of the woodland. But we chose a straight (well straight-ish!) walk from Pontneddfechan to the car park at Cwm Porth (which hangs above a spectacular cave system – but more of that later).

If you know this area then it may surprise you that we haven't included the most famous waterfall found here, Sgwd Yr Eira. It's a lovely waterfall that comes with the added attraction of allowing people to walk under – that is behind – the water! Unfortunately for us though, it was closed to the public when we visited (there had been some rock falls and the various agencies responsible for the rivers and the wildlife here had to make it safe again). At the time of writing, the falls are open again but you should always phone ahead and check just in case. If they're closed, then there a number of trails that the Centre staff can recommend to you – and it's these that form the basis of our walk.

Our route starts off from the car park near the Angel Inn, just across the road from the Waterfall Centre. A very 'municipal-style' set of low park

The Horseshoe Falls.

gates leads you into waterfall country and there's a big information board at the top of the path to help guide you through. But while it tells you lots about the birds and wildlife you'll see on your journey, it doesn't tell you anything about the ground under your feet. And on this walk a little knowledge of geology goes a long way. For example underneath that notice

board is the Farewell Rock – a band of sandstone that marks the end of the productive seams in the South Wales coalfield. It got its name from the miners who knew that when they hit it, it was farewell to the coal and time to start digging somewhere else.

Further along the path, that sandstone punches through the ground in a rocky ridge to your left, just behind the trees. As you wander, it pays to keep in mind that all this peaceful, woodland beauty (and the sparkling, restful waterfalls that accompany it) is all here because of huge seismic activity and some serious geological violence.

Similarly the flat, straight, easy path you take for the first section of the walk is another by-product of the area's rich mineral heritage. It's a former tramway for the nearby Silica mines. In fact at some points you'll still see the old stone sleepers that supported the track, with the holes at each end that secured the rails. As such, this first section is very easy to do and it also attracts wheelchair users and cyclists (as well as families with kids in push chairs too). Silica rock or quartzite, is a hard rock composed of silicon dioxide (quartz to you or I) which has very few impurities and a very high melting point. During the Industrial Revolution it was used to make firebricks for use in furnaces and exported all over the world. In Russia, for example, fire bricks are known as Dinas, the name coming from the Dinas rock here in the Pontneddfechan, which was mined from the late 18th century right up until 1964.

Today the remains of the old levels and tramways can still be seen and you'll pass a couple of these small 'pillar and stalled' tunnels as you make your way towards the first waterfall. You get to that by crossing a short wooden bridge to the left side of the river, following the signs for Sgwd Gwladus (or the Waterfall of the Chieftain). If you hadn't crossed the bridge then the path would have taken you to a viewing point (with bench) on the opposite side of the bank. It's a nice spot but our route allows you to walk up close to the falls which then tower above you.

The falls are named after the beautiful young daughter of Brychan of Brycheiniog (yes, the same 5th century Welsh king who was father to Dwynwen – and allegedly 22 other girls too). Gwladus shared her sister's luck when it came to love, falling for a young man called Einion. Their relationship was not allowed to flourish however which broke the poor girl's heart. Succumbing to a debilitating sadness, both she and Einion were mysteriously immortalised, transformed into two waterfalls. His is further up-stream, a 70-foot fall into a pool in the River Pryddin, although unlike Gwladus there is no clear path to it.

The quirk of the story, of course, is that although the two could not be together in this life, they are now truly inseparable, their spirits flowing together for all eternity, over the rocks and into the waters of the pool below Sgwd Gwladus. For those of you who do not share this romantic notion a geologist will tell you that the waterfall is a classic case of sandstone over-laying a seam of softer mud rock shale. The shale is more susceptible to the abrasion of the water and is worn away much faster than the tougher harder sandstone. This continues until the sandstone is left unsupported and collapses, making the waterfall, before the process starts again. A quick calculation by our guide led to an estimated movement of 1.3 metres every 1,000 years. In other words that big waterfall is reversing up the gorge at a rate of about one millimetre every year. So one of nature's least spectacular geological attractions then! Sgwd Gwladus (which is also known as the Angel falls and the Lady falls) is a suitably impressive waterfall, carved into a natural black rock basin that borders the pool on the far shore. On the path side there is a shallow shale beach leading down to the water, while its misty micro-climate means it's full of ferns and mosses, making for a lush and, when the waters are in full flow, fairly loud bolt hole.

Take the path up the bank to the top of the waterfall and you get some more geological jiggery pokery. The first, if the waters have receded enough to allow you to see it, is a series of plant fossils set into the polished rock of the head of the waterfall. If it's not too slippery you can get onto the rock and take a look at the fossils (but remember, just be careful if you do decide to do this).

From here you head back down the bank and follow the signs for the Horseshoe Falls. The walk now takes you over the up and down bounce of a typical gorge path and – depending on the weather – it can either be close and humid here or muddy and wet. Occasionally the elements combine to make it shaded and cool too, so it's not all bad!

The river and path begin to open out as you approach falls number two. These are the gorgeous Horseshoe Falls, a series of sinking, semi-circular half moon pools. A triple tiered treat, they are flanked by oak trees which are an indicator of the acidic soil here. At this point the gorge opens out and the waters here seem to luxuriate in the change in light and space. Make the most of it. The trees will close in again from here and you have some tricky, potentially slippery climbs ahead of you as the path begins to rise.

Again, the rocks here can be exposed when the river level drops and some walkers are tempted to walk across them up to the bottom of the next falls (rather than get the view from the main path, which is set to the side of the gorge and higher up). On the days we walked through here that was impossible (the rain put paid to that idea) but if you are tempted and conditions allow then please be careful. It's a treacherous journey and you can easily turn an ankle or worse.

The third fall, Sgwd y Dwilli, is a five minute walk from the Horseshoe and with that one under your belt, it's a long and sometimes tricky trudge up to Sgwd Dwilli Uchaf.

This is a gentle waterfall which once doubled as picturesque Exmoor for a BBC adaptation of *Lorna Doone*. It's a magical place, wooded but with a wall of white water to lift the shade, and is another of those Tolkien-esque pockets of the real world which one can imagine was once the abode of mystics and warriors. Legend has it that a cave somewhere in this forest leads to the world of faeries. If you find it and get through, the lands of Lord Oberon and Queen Titania will probably look like this.

From here you press on to the car park and picnic area at Pont Melin Fach. Some people end the walk here and arrange to be picked up and taken back to the village of Pontneddfechan, or walk back to the start (and if you just do that, then you will have completed the National Park's 'Elidir Trail'). Of course we continued on and from the picnic area we hit the tarmac and took the main road, aiming for our final falls, Sgwd Uchaf Clun Gwyn. To get there you rise above the gorge and onto the sheep-grazed hills above. You pass an old petrol station and shop (and an all too rare public phone box) before dropping back down into the trees again. Of course you will have no doubt

worked out that with a straightforward arrangement of transport at the various car parks, you could drive this bit of the journey, but however you get there, the final falls is worth the trip.

This is Sgwd Uchaf Clun Gwyn or the Higher Waterfall of the White Meadow. There are wooden steps that zig zag down from the well-marked path to the top of the waterfall, and at all points down, it offers you some fantastic views. The path leads you to the waters edge but please be careful, you are walking close to wet rock – and that's wet rock that leads to a bone-breaking drop just yards from the path.

If it's safe and you can explore that rock's surface, you'll see the fossilised roots of tree that grew here during the Carboniferous period, when this area was a tropical rainforest (making them around 318 million years old – so they are older than the dinosaurs).

If you still feel the need to track down even more waterfalls then a trail here will branch off and take you to Sgwd Isaf Clun Gwyn and further down Sgwd Pannwr, but for us five was enough. And when a walker tires of waterfalls it's time to go home, so we then followed the Mellte river up to Cwm Porth.

The river flattens out here and slows at the top of the gorge. Before too long you'll arrive at a place called the Blue Pool, which is the point where the Mellte emerges from under the ground.

It's at this point that the river disappears on its subterranean route where we finish our walk. Cwm Porth is a car park with a National Parks office and little else, yet it's always busy. The reason? It's also home to Porth yr Ogof, a cave you reach by a steep, rutted and – yes – slippery path that takes you down to the bank of the river. There you'll see the huge entrance to the cave – a massive gaping maw and one of the biggest in Wales. Have a look, take a picture – but if you're tempted inside, seek out a guide. Because while the cave is a magnet for school trips (and parties of supervised school children provide an endless procession in and out of the cave) don't underestimate it. It's a complex cave system used by serious cavers, full of tunnels and passages.

And then there's the river. Mellte is Welsh for lightning, and it earned that name for the speed at which this river will swell and flood through here and into those dark chambers. Frankly you're better off sticking to the waterfalls – although the cave does add a stunning footnote to this special geologically themed walk and if nothing else, Porth yr Ogof proves Wales is just as interesting and beautiful below ground as it is above it.

Merthyr Mawr

Near: Bridgend

Ordnance Survey Grid Reference SS 872772

OS Explorer Map 151

Derek says...

This walk is a hidden treasure with spectacular views, mysterious legends and one of the biggest sand dune systems in the world. It's also got great beaches, rugged coastal paths and the spooky ruins of Candleston Castle – all just a stone's throw from the A48.

If you're a romantic like me, you will love the picturesque village of Merthyr Mawr with its collection of thatched cottages. The Sahara-like sand dunes which surround it are an important wildlife habitat, supporting a rich variety of plants. Parts of the Hollywood blockbuster *Lawrence of Arabia* were filmed here. If you're feeling fit, why not run up the 'Big Dipper', the second biggest sand dune in Europe – and the starting point of the Merthyr Mawr Christmas Pudding 10km Challenge!

Try not to get your toes wet when crossing the stepping stones over the River Ewenny to Ogmore Castle and look out for the awesome view across Dunraven Bay. Look for fossils on the beach, but watch the tide.

If time allows, nip into the Dunraven Bay Heritage Coast Centre where you can find out more information about this beautiful part of Wales.

Starting from the ruins of Candleston Castle, the first part of the walk takes in the second highest sand dune system in Europe, the picturesque village of Merthyr Mawr and Ogmore Castle. Remember to check the high tide times if you're planning to cross River Ewenny at the stepping stones – it's a long walk round if you get it wrong!

A gentle walk along the river leads you into Ogmore-by-Sea. Here, the landscape starts to take on a much harsher aspect; as you approach Southerndown the distinctive 'banding' of the cliffs is dramatically revealed.

Whatever the weather, walking along these cliffs and through Dunraven Park is an uplifting experience, finishing with what Derek said was one of 'the best views in Wales'.

This coast has been part of my life, since childhood. but it never fails to surprise and inspire me.

Belinda Ashong

The Glamorgan Heritage Coast is yet another demonstration of how much neglected splendour we have in Wales. Neglected in the sense that this eye-popping stretch of coastline lies between two big centres of population – Cardiff and Bridgend – yet it's remarkably light on walkers' foot traffic.

In fact most people who head for this area make for the beach resort of Porthcawl, and are largely unaware of the kind of fantastic scenery just a mile or so from the famous caravan park at Trecco Bay. But if they were to swap their flip-flops for a pair of walking boots, they'd find a place that was a magical mix of chocolate box villages, mammoth sand dune systems, two castles, some awe-inspiring cliffs and a coastline view which many believe to be the best in Wales.

To give you a full flavour of what's on offer, we took two short walks and jammed them together to make a marathon seven mile hike that delivers around four hours of rambling pleasure.

It starts off in the car park at Candlestone, which gives you access straight onto the dune system of Merthyr Mawr Warren. Before you hit the sand, however, hang back and take a detour through the ruins of Candlestone Castle.

Strictly speaking a fortified manor house rather than a castle, it was the 14th century home of the de Cantelupe family. In truth, it's not the most exciting of castles, but you can wander through the main courtyard, and while the ivy-covered ruins are fenced off from the public, you can make out the remains of the main house. You should also be able to spot a particularly fine 15th century fireplace in the Hall block which backs on to the main tower (a tower that stands almost eight metres tall). There's a fence here vto keep inquisitive visitors away from the crumbling façade (so it's for the ruin's protection as well as for walkers) but you can clamber through the undergrowth and look behind the castle and into the inner workings of the house, all from a safe distance.

Nowadays Candleston is a home for some roosting bats and not much else, but at one time it was the centre of the busy little village of Tregawntlo (or Treganllaw), although nothing remains of it now. The village was swallowed by the sands when the dunes began a remorseless advance on the site during the Middle Ages. The image of the castle left standing among the windswept trees – the last trace of a lost community – is an eerie one and not surprisingly, there are several ghost stories associated with the ruin.

One story tells of travellers being waylaid here at night by an apparition that seized them and dragged them off to an old tombstone, forcing the frightened captives to touch it, whereupon their hands would become trapped in the headstone's intricate carvings. Their only way of escaping this trap was to pray, and their predicament may have something to do with the legend that the castle was built on the site of an old Celtic church.

Once free of the clutches of Candleston, you wander downhill and through the shaded tracks of the forest, before being confronted by the Big Dipper. This is not some errant attraction from the nearby fun fair at Porthcawl but a huge steep-sided hill of sand. It's our chosen way into the amazing dune system of Merthyr Mawr Warren, and while it's not the only route in (so if you don't fancy the climb, don't worry), it is a famous challenge for local walkers and fitness fanatics alike.

The dune system once stretched all the way to the Mumbles in Swansea, and these days is a National Nature Reserve. The Dipper is the second highest dune in Europe and the unforgiving slope is a magnet for amateur runners and professional sportspeople alike. Over the years the odd Olympic athlete has trained here – including, local legend has it, Steve Ovett – while the Welsh rugby team have also been put through their

paces on the big hill. It's also the start point for the annual Merthyr Mawr Christmas Pudding race – a 'fun run' organised each December by Bridgend Athletic club that also includes a circuit of the nearby Southerndown Golf Course. Competitors who complete the 10 km course get a Christmas Pudding – hence the name!

Five minutes of hard walking will get you to the brow of the Big Dipper, and from here you'll get a fantastic view of about two thirds of the walk ahead. Looking back to your left, you'll see Candlestone's ruins, while to the right of that, you'll spot the other castle on the walk – Ogmore. You'll also get a great view of the vast dune system you're about to enter.

Dune system suggests a 'Sahara-like' expanse of yellow sand, but even though in the 60s it was used as a location for the film *Lawrence of Arabia*, this is not a desert landscape. Rather it's a real oasis for wildlife, a place packed with plants, awash with greenery and bristling with life. It's a vibrant, colourful ecosystem and if the weather warms early in spring, then this is a great place for a wildflower walk. Quite simply there is too much here to list; suffice to say that in spring you'll see yellow carpets of Bird's Foot Trefoil and Biting Stonecrop, which in summer will segue into the pink spread of Rest Harrow. In the drier sites, Bee and Pyramidal orchids and wispy green Tway Blade mix with the ruby reds of early Marsh orchids (in the damper areas) and the tall spikes of yellow Evening Primrose and the blue Vipers Bugloss. You'll find odd little plants

like moonwort, a primitive small fern, and rare in much of south Wales, while dune pansies, dog violets, eyebrights and milkwort all vie for your attention.

Many of these plants thrive because of the rabbits that live in the Warren. They eat some of the grasses and vegetation that would otherwise out-compete the smaller, more vulnerable plants for space. You'll see the odd bunny as you wander around, although they aren't as abundant as they once were, and their voracious appetites almost caused the destruction of nearby Merthyr Mawr. In the 1840s, they left the vegetation so threadbare and damaged that sandstorms threatened to engulf the village. Disaster was only averted through the mass planting of sea buckthorn bushes which stabilised the dunes and stopped the sand drifting in. However, such is

the topsy-turvy nature of the struggle for natural dominance here that the dunes themselves are now under threat from the buckthorn, which at one point covered over 25 acres in a single thorny mass of vegetation. Since the 1980s though, local nature conservation agencies have responded to the spikey threat with regular attacks, cutting and burning the plants to maintain the natural balance and free up the dunes. As such you'll regularly come across huge mounds of bleached buckthorn branches ready for burning, stretched out on the sand like the carcass of some washed-up primordial beast.

Bizarrely, the buckthorn did once come to the aid of the rabbits that it was introduced to combat in the first place. During the last myxomatosis outbreaks (which devastated similar rabbit populations in places like Kenfig, just a mile or two down the coast), the numbers of rabbits at Merthyr Mawr remained relatively healthy and robust. Because they tended to use the buckthorn for cover, they spent more time above ground, so limiting the chances of picking up the fleas which were the main carriers of the disease.

The real wildlife success story, though, is the large numbers and varieties of insects. This is reckoned to be the best insect hunting habitat in Wales with a fantastic array of snails, wasps, bees, moths and butterflies (like the brilliantly named brimstone and grizzled skipper butterflies). Obviously, the more abundant the wild flowers, the more abundant the insect life, and in turn bird life.

With the bewildering array of trails and bridleways criss-crossing the dunes, it's easy to get lost, and spend a whole morning exploring here. If you do, you may find signs of human history too. For example, there is a Napoleonic shooting range tucked away in the trees, about a mile from the car park, as well as the remains of much older human use of the landscape (evidence of Mesolithic, Neolithic, early Bronze and Iron Age habitation has also been discovered here).

But if you do find yourself wandering off the beaten path and losing your way, just head for the nearest high dune that crests the treeline, and look for the castle ruins. Once sighted, it will give you a bearing that will see you steer a straight course through the twists and turns of the Warren, and on towards the village of Merthyr Mawr.

The first building you'll see is the church of St Teilo, which was built in 1850 on the site of an earlier Medieval church, the foundations of which can still be seen today. The churchyard has an embarrassment of riches when it comes to crooked crosses and weathered headstones, and its crisp Victorian styling is the perfect introduction to the village itself. Merthyr Mawr is arguably one of the prettiest places in Wales. It's a collection of 'chocolate box' thatched cottages congregated around a small village green, and it looks almost too good to be true – like you've stumbled across a film set or a particularly authentic theme park.

The village has two bridges – a white wooden bridge that leads you out of Merthyr Mawr and on towards Ogmore, and a stone one, as you enter from the main road. The stone bridge is known as the

Dipping Bridge because local farmers would push their sheep through the holes in the parapets for their annual wash in the river. The second bridge looks a little like a mini-Severn Crossing and has the local nickname of 'the bouncing bridge'. To find out why, just stop in the middle of it and jump up and down. Guess what happens? (Yup, it bounces).

Cross it and head past the ponies grazing in the fields behind the low stone walls and you'll get your first glimpse of Ogmore Castle. To get to the castle, you have to cross over a series of 42 stepping stones that poke out of the river bed. They're fairly hefty square slabs of rock, and as long as the tide is out, they shouldn't hold too many problems for you. Once you're safely across, you're free to explore the castle itself.

The fortress dates back to 1116, when Glamorgan was ruled by the Normans. Established by William de Londres, the first castle here was an earthwork, but subsequent re-inforcement of the site produced a far more impressive and sturdy structure, the remains of which still stand today.

The Great Tower, probably built by William's son Maurice, is the most impressive part of the ruin, and it once stood three storeys high (around 40 feet). Most of the other construction at Ogmore dates to the 13th century, and maybe due to its dominant position and threatening walls, it was not a place that saw much 'action' and it ceased to have any military purpose by the late Middle Ages.

Like Candleston, there are a few legends associated with the ruin – the favourite being the story of how Maurice de Londres was forced to hand over some of his stolen lands back to the local Welsh.

The Norman lords enjoyed extensive hunting grounds in the area but demanded that all game be left for them and them alone. Obviously the locals, who were often on the point of starvation, would turn to poaching to feed their families and before long one man was caught and sentenced to death. Maurice's daughter asked, for a birthday present, that the man be pardoned and that a section of land be set aside for the people of the area to use as their own. William agreed, on condition that whatever land was given back should be no more than the area that she could walk around barefoot before sundown. At the end of her walk she had marked out a stretch of land that became Southerndown Common and which is common land even to this day.

The castle also marks the end of the first of the two walks that we have joined together and it's also a place where you can grab some refreshments – either in the nearby tearoom, or at the historic (and oddly named) pub, The Pelican in Her Piety.

Press on though, and pass the confluence of the rivers Ogmore and Ewenny, then head down the estuary towards the coastal path. As you hit the sea, look back to your right and take in another view of that massive dune system, while further up the coast you also see the caravan site at Trecco Bay which, if the sun is shining, shimmers like a big silver beach in the distance.

From this point, you head for the seashore, and there are dozens of caves and rock pools to catch your eye. We pressed on, though, and got to the higher coastal path as soon as possible, giving us more time for the beach and views at the end of the walk. Once on the cliffs, you'll see few fellow walkers, and with mostly sheep for company, it's wise to pay heed to the warning signs, and stay well away from the edge – however spectacular the views are from there!

Half an hour's walk will soon find you descending onto Southerndown beach. It's a great bucket and spade spot (when the tide's out, that is – when it's in, the sea water is almost in the car park) and as it's a west-facing beach, it's also a magnet for surfers (the offshore wind from the east brewing up much good quality surf).

It's also a Mecca for Doctor Who fans, as it has

twice doubled for Bad Wolf Bay in the series (a Norwegian beach in an Earth from a parallel universe, where the Doctor's companion Rose was left behind by the Tardis). There are pictures of the cast and crew filming at Southerndown in the nearby visitor centre, but for a really out-of-this-world experience, you need to ignore the beach and walk through the grand double gates adjacent to the seafront car park.

These used to guard the entrance to Dunraven Castle, a former grand manor house, built on the headland that separates the popular Southerndown from its much larger sister beach. To get to it you have to climb the hill towards the ruins of Dunraven, passing the house's pretty hidden gardens. It only takes a slight detour to take in both ruins and gardens, although you'll probably want to visit them either side of the walk's stunning finale. The house itself was built in 1802 and demolished in the 1960s, and there is little to see of it today, bar some walls and the exposed foundations (ironically much more remains of both Ogmore and Candleston castles).

The first fortress was built here in 1130, when the land was given as a reward to a gallant steward who had organised a successful defence of Ogmore Castle. A band of raiders had attacked while William was away with his men, leaving Arnold Botiler to master the stronghold's defences. When his lord returned, he was so impressed with his steward's actions that he knighted the man. He gave Arnold the headland on the proviso that if William ever visited, he had to be offered three cups of wine. Obviously he agreed to this fairly lenient tenure and today his family, now known as Butler, carry a triumvirate of cups on their family crest. Not only that, but there's also a local pub named the Three Golden Cups not far from Southerndown beach itself.

But while Arnold's story survives, his home does not. It only made it as far as the 15th century, when Owain Glyndŵr razed it to the ground. Various prominent owners took over the land here and built impressive homes, but the last mansion to occupy this prominent spot was Dunraven. It was built by the Wyndham family, who lavished attention on it, remodelling it extensively throughout the 1800s. However, by the 20th century it fell into disrepair, finally becoming ruined before being demolished in 1962.

If you want to see what's left of the mansion,

then take a look at it as you head back at the end of your walk, where the elevated position gives you a great view of the final leg of the route, as well as great views of the beach.

The garden is best visited on the way to the top. That way, walkers get the benefit of the walls, built to shelter the plants from the cruel sea winds. You enter it through a wooden door in the wall, and once inside you'll find four well-maintained themed gardens, which provide a real contrast to everything else on the walk. It's like stepping into a Victorian fantasy and a world of garden parties, secret meetings, posh frocks and quiet intrigue. The garden is divided into four sections – a Victorian garden, a fruit garden, a plant hunters' garden and a Tudor or herb garden – and it also includes the remains of an ice house. The tranquil surroundings and the colourful scented path make for a gentle climb to the top of the headland. It also means that the final section of the walk comes as a (pleasant) shock.

Exiting the garden through a picnic area, you are immediately directed straight to the fenced-off edge of the cliff path. From the ornate cultivation of the Victorian garden, you are now confronted by the awesome sight of a landscape smashed and sculpted by massive earth movement and the constant savage battering of the sea. This is a view that has been literally millions of years in the making, and it goes without saying that it's simply stunning. From the viewing point here, it stretches endlessly away into the distance, an unbroken line of tumbling cliff tops drawing your eye to the horizon.

From here you can appreciate just how vast the beach is, stretching as it does all the way down to Nash Point near Llantwit Major. From this high vantage point, you can appreciate the jumble of faults and folds in the exposed rock face, a juddering pile-up of cliff face that decorates the beach with the debris of smashed and shattered slabs of stone.

The cliffs here are Liassic limestone which is around 180 million years old, and is sandwiched between soft shale which makes for a very unstable combination – hence the cliff collapses. Unsurprisingly, this is an area that offers a feast for fossil hunters but be warned, if you want to go hunting for them, you are not allowed to tap into the cliff walls to free them. Instead just try and pick through the rubble on the beach for your finds. Of course, the best place to go looking for these fossils is right under the cliffs, which isn't really the safest place to be, considering how unstable they are.

To get down to the beach you take a series of steps that lead you straight onto the natural stone slab below. The beach is a real treat. For a start, you can only get to it by foot, so it's a paradise reserved exclusively for walkers, and often you'll have this seemingly endless section of coastline to yourself. As such you're left free to marvel at the crumpled cliffs, clamber over the fallen stones, fish for crabs in the rock pools, and walk the thin strip of sand before sticking a thirsty toe in the sea water.

And the only drawback to all this splendid isolation? You have to be accountable for your own safety. This magnificent scenery comes with a warning, because here you are at the mercy of the Bristol tidal channel, the second highest tidal range in the world. So check the tide times and keep an eye on the approaching wash of the waves, as this is not a place to be caught out – and chances are, there would be few witnesses to your plight if you were to get into difficulty. In other words, don't expect a shout of warning, or to have a good Samaritan within earshot should you find yourself in trouble.

But approached with the right degree of caution and a sensible outlook, this is a stunning place to spend some time and is a fitting finale to a really epic walk (and it is epic, the word count on my PC tells me so – it's the longest chapter in the book). But the Glamorgan Heritage Coast is such a rich and rewarding landscape to explore, that any walk here will leave you breathless and hungry for more. So whether taken as two separate routes or as one long marathon wander, this is the perfect introduction to an often ignored area of Wales. I hope it whets your appetite.

Y Lliwedd

Near: Llanberis

Ordnance Survey Grid Reference SH 618507

OS Explorer Map OL17

Derek says...

I've been up Snowdon a few times, but never by this beautiful, quiet route which starts at the Nantgwynant car park. The route is easy to follow along most of its length, but you need to be in good shape as it can be strenuous. There are some dangerous crags, cliffs and steep drops – also loose scree which can become slippery in rain.

So, be prepared with suitable footwear, waterproofs, warm clothing, a hat, gloves, food and drink, a survival bag, map and compass. People have 'come a cropper' – so mind how you go, especially in bad weather.

Along the way, you will pass Gladstone Rock, old slate mines, rocky spoil heaps and some lovely waterfalls where you can cool down on a hot summer's day. Scenes from *Carry On Up the Khyber* were filmed here too.

Unfortunately, we didn't make it to the top of Y Lliwedd as the weather took a turn for the worse, but the views were fantastic overlooking Glaslyn and Llyn Llydaw. If you have time, pop into the Caffi Gwynant (Gwynant Café) located near the base of the Watkin Path. It's an ideal place for a drink or bite to eat, before or after your walk.

The Watkin Path was dedicated to the public in 1893 by the landowner Sir Edward Watkin, with a rousing speech by William Gladstone. The path winds its way through deciduous broadleaved woodland, passing the Afon Cwm Llan waterfalls and Gladstone Rock.

The cliffs of Lliwedd have drawn botanists searching for rare alpine plants and lichens, and rock climbers in the 18th and 19th centuries. These were the training grounds for the mountaineers on the successful 1953 Everest expedition.

The weather can change very rapidly, and it is important to ensure you feel fit enough and are prepared with sufficient skills and equipment to navigate the sometimes exposed scrambling towards the summit.

With good weather, you will be rewarded with fine views of Snowdonia's mountain peaks, Cardigan Bay and Cadair Idris.

Nikki Wallis

Warden, Snowdonia National Park

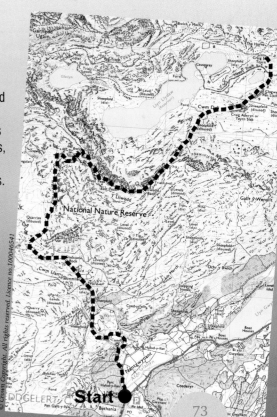

73

If one programme in the TV series spelt out the pleasure and the pain of walking in Wales, it was this one. It was the only walk we failed to complete, as we were beaten back from the summit by a combination of wind, rain, freezing cold and thick, thick fog – and we were doing the walk in July too!

The plan had been to take the Watkin Path (which is one of the more demanding routes up Snowdon) and then head for Y Lliwedd (the third highest peak in the Horseshoe) before coming down the other side of the mountain, past the lakes and ending up at Pen-y-pas (the famous Snowdon mountain centre).

However plans have a habit of changing fast when you're out and about around Snowdon. For a start, it's one of the wettest places in Britain and has an annual rainfall of around 4,500 millilitres (that's 180 inches of water in old money!). Whichever way you look at it, this is not the place to visit without a waterproof coat of some description. Also because of its height and topography, Snowdon enjoys its own micro-climate – so one side can be bathed in sunshine while another side can be experiencing a downpour. Add to that the risk of cold weather at altitude, the wind chill factor and the

threat of low cloud and mist and you have a potentially lethal cocktail for outdoors enthusiasts. The watchword for Snowdon is caution.

And the best advice is that whatever your plans are, be prepared to change them – as our guide sagely remarked: 'Getting to the top of a climb isn't compulsory but getting down is!'.

So now that we've scared you and sent you scurrying for your wellies and raincoat, it's worth pointing out that Snowdon is as good as walking country gets in the UK, and this route is a great alternative to actually scaling the main peak.

It gives you a taste of everything that this range has to offer. You get to walk through beautiful wooded glades, gorgeous pasture and the brooding spoils of the slate tips. You'll see waterfalls and lakes and you'll wander through the relics of the area's industrial past while hitting one stunning view after another in an endless procession to the top of the ridge.

From there, you'll have a chance to try your hand at a bit of rock

scrambling and – if you're brave enough – to experience one of those dizzying death-defying drops that are usually the preserve of climbers.

Finally, as Snowdon (or Yr Wyddfa as it's known in Welsh) will always be a magnet for walkers and tourists, this route will always guarantee you peace, quiet, and the freedom to enjoy the spectacular countryside without tripping over school parties and picnicking holidaymakers.

Y Lliwedd is about 600 feet shorter than Snowdon (which hits a towering 1,085 metres or 3,560 feet high) but it still provides a lofty vantage point from which to take in the natural wonders around you. In fact, the north face (the steep, near-vertical drop where the mountain falls to the lake below) is a testing ground for many experienced climbers. It was first explored in the late 19th century, and in 1909 was the subject of the first British climbing guide, *The Climbs on Lliwedd*, by J M A Thomson and A W Andrews, while the noted British climber George Mallory undertook many of his early climbs here.

Before you make the peak, though, you have a lot of walking to do and it starts at the Nantgwynant Car Park on the A498. Cross the road here and take the signs for the Watkin Path which is one of seven classic routes to the peak of Snowdon (the other six being the Pyg Track, the Llanberris Track, the Miner's Track, the Rhyd Ddu Track and the Snowdon Ranger and the Snowdon Horseshoe).

The Watkin Path is special in a few ways. For many walkers this is one of the most demanding routes up the mountain because of the length and the height gained from bottom top. The car park stands at just 57 metres above sea level, so for Y Lliwedd you have to make an 850 metre ascent, which added to the nine-mile route we're following, makes for a fair old hike.

It's special for those with a sense of history too, because this was one of the first dedicated public footpaths in Britain. Sir William Watkin, who commissioned the path and opened it to the public, was a former entrepreneur, business tycoon, railway magnate and Liberal MP who owned a retirement chalet below Snowdon in Cwm y Llan. You pass the ruined remains of that chalet as you walk through the rhododendron and oak-filled first section. There's not much to see now, just an old cooker and a tumble of bricks, although a more impressive memorial to Sir Watkin awaits further into the climb. But the path that he had laid out is easy to follow and has benefited over the years from regular upgrades, so that when you get above the treeline towards the tumbling waters of the Afon Cwm Llan, you are walking on a hefty carpet of rock that guides you right into the heart of the mountain.

Even if you walked this section alone, as far as the waterfall and rock pool at the top of the pass, you'd be rewarded with beautiful scenery and great views – but there's so much more to come. Beyond the waterfall you'll see the remains of an old water wheel and, if you're lucky, you'll catch sight of a dipper, a small brown bird that ducks under the water to fish for food.

Crossing a flat bridge of weathered sleepers bordered by one of the area's trademark tombstone trails of slate-tile fencing, you pass the ruins of some old slate quarry buildings (some pock-marked with bullet holes, where soldiers used them for target practice back in the 40s).

As you leave the shell of the buildings behind, you then head toward Gladstone's rock. This is a huge slab of stone inlaid with a plaque that commemorates the dedication service held here back in 1892, when the 83-year-old prime minister William Gladstone officially opened the Watkin Path before a crowd of over 2,000 dignitaries, locals and well-wishers. And if you're wondering how the venerable octogenarian PM made it up this far, be assured that he arrived at the rock in some style – on a horse and carriage brought in to spare him the steep climb.

From here you begin to enter quarrying country, as the path takes you through some of the old South Snowdon slateworks. The most obvious building is the tall-walled barracks which used to house the slateworkers (the men slept here during the week before returning home at the weekend). Below them lie the dressing sheds and workshops, while on the slopes to your right, you'll easily make out the old tramline that took slate down the mountain to the villages below.

The huge mounds of slate waste and the barren barracks make for a good place to stop and take a breather. You get a good view of the job ahead, although some walkers heading for Snowdon take this staging post as an opportunity to 'scope out' alternative routes to the top. That's not such a wise exercise, because although you can spot what look like a dozen or so alternative and seemingly easier or shorter tracks from here, don't be tempted. These trails aren't so easy to follow once you're on them.

To complicate matters further the sheep make their own idiosyncratic (and downright dangerous) tracks up and down here and if you make a mistake and start following one of those routes, you're in for trouble. So keep it simple and stick with the official path and follow the natural rock road to the top.

From the spoils of the slate tip, the path begins a steep zig-zag climb to the summit of the ridge, and from here you'll really feel the grind of the mountain as you twist and turn through the ever more demanding gradient. While the terrain will make you breathe hard, it's not that tough a walk, providing you are fit and properly equipped (you really shouldn't do any walk like this without good boots, for example). And on every day that we walked the Watkin Path while making the programme, we saw people of all ages, from grandmothers to grandchildren all happily coping with the climb.

To put it simply, if you're sensible, it's there to be enjoyed. And the biggest part of that enjoyment comes from the views here.

As the path clings to your left, you'll see Yr Aran to your right, a pyramid peak that looks impressively high. However, just remind yourself that at 747 metres, it stands 141 metres short of the peak you're heading for! You'll also get great views out towards the Irish Sea and of Dolgellau to the south, while above you lies Bwlch y Saethau – the Pass of Arrows.

This is where the mountain's Arthurian heritage begins to play into the walk. The pass was allegedly the scene of King Arthur's last battle, and the spot where he lay mortally wounded and asked Sir Bedwyr (or if you prefer, Bedivere) to take his sword Excalibur from him and throw it into the waters of Glaslyn. In another legend, that dangerous north cliff face of Y Lliwedd that you're heading towards is supposed to hide a cave where Arthur's knights sleep until their country needs them again and their leader calls them forth.

As we get to the crest of the ridge, we finally leave the Watkin Path, which continues to your left towards Snowdon, and we head right to join the Horseshoe track, which will lead us over the peaks and down to the lakeside, eventually

terminating at Pen-y-Pas.

Before you set off though, stand along that ridge which curls from peak to peak and take in the scene below you – you've earned it. It's one of the great mountain views in Wales, with the lakes Llyn Teyrn and the larger Llyn Llydaw and Glaslyn stretched out before you, Pen-y-Pas in the distance and the silvery paths of the Pyg Track and the Miner's Track tracing their way up the sides of the mountain toward Snowdon. You also get a good look at the summit of Snowdon although that's best viewed from the peak of Y Lliwedd – which is where you head next.

The following section of the walk is the most challenging as you begin to scramble and climb up the ridge. There is an easier, slightly gentler route which tacks along up the back of the slope but if you want something more 'mountain' then stick with the ridge route. Whichever way you go, though, be warned: the bare rock here can be slippery in damp conditions, so take your time and take care.

Also be aware of the edge. That may sound stupidly obvious but in the wrong conditions, keeping on the path is the difference between making it home or facing a call-out from the local mountain rescue team. In fact, it was at this point on our televised walk that we had to turn back. Wind, rain and – more tellingly – thick mist, made this part of the mountain too dangerous to continue, so we reluctantly headed back to the car park at Nantgwynant.

Had we been able to continue then we would have walked along the ridge down to Lliwedd Bach and then slowly off the mountain to the side of the lake. If you do get to see the lake up close, then maybe you'll agree that it is hard to imagine this as the home of the Lady of the Lake. It's probably more likely that Camlan Valley in Merionydd has the best claim to being Arthur's final resting place (just don't mention that to the pro-Snowdon Arthurians!).

From there we would have passed this bleak stretch of water, with the dilapidated ruins of more mining buildings on the far shore, before crossing to the Miner's track side of the mountain and walking the final mile to the Mountain Centre. Had we been able to film the complete route we would have returned home with a wonderful advert for this Mecca of British walking, with the view back to the famous Horseshoe as good as it gets – as it really does show off everything that the area has to offer. As it was, we were just happy to get home!

Just take our experience as a cautionary warning, make the right preparations, take the right precautions then get out and about on this magnificent mountain. You won't be disappointed.

Llangollen

Near: Llangollen

Ordnance Survey Grid Reference SJ 215522

OS Explorer Map 215

Derek says...

Llangollen is a lovely market town in the Dee Valley with over 3,000 years of history, making it well worth a visit. It's famous for its steam railway, hot-air balloon fiesta and the international musical eisteddfod – but it's also a great place to go walking. In fact, one of the best ways of discovering this part of Wales is on foot.

This easy-to-follow trail has stunning views, unspoilt countryside and a wealth of wildlife. It starts off in the town centre and takes you on a circuit passing some wonderful sights. Stroll along the Llangollen Canal and have a picnic near the Horseshoe Falls. Pop into Llantysilio Church where you can pray for good weather and have a gander at the rare medieval oak eagle lectern. Afterwards, take some time to enjoy the tranquility of Valle Crucis Abbey.

Look out for Velvet Hill, which gets its name from the soft texture of the grass and moss. Its Welsh name, Coed Hyrddyn, means 'wood of the long man'. It's a steep climb up to Castell Dinas Bran, known as Crow Castle (1,062 feet), but the views from the top take your breath away. The Pontcysyllte Aqueduct, which carries the Llangollen Canal 126 feet above the River Dee, is the tallest and longest navigable aqueduct in the world!

This walk is simply stunning: stunning views, stunning history, stunning ruins.

You'll be hard pressed not to fall in love with the area after completing this route, which takes you out of the picturesque town of Llangollen and on a historical walk through the ages.

The route follows the towpath of Telford's canal, which is still used by horse-drawn boats! After passing the Horseshoe Falls – a semi-circular weir also designed by Telford – the path meanders uphill over to Valle Crucis Abbey. The last part of the walk involves a long climb up to the romantic ruins of Dinas Brân Castle, but it's worth it. Sit back and enjoy the breathtaking views across the Dee Valley.

Samantha Williams
Denbighshire Council

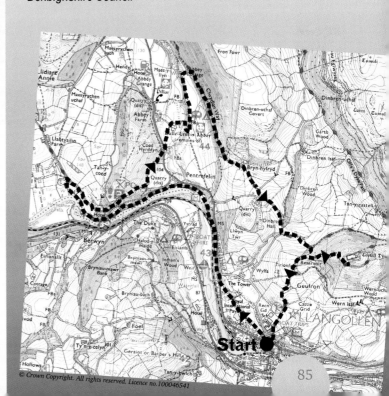

85

EVERY July, Llangollen opens its doors to the world, with the annual International Eisteddfod turning over the town's streets to crowds of music lovers and performers from all corners of the globe.

The festival, which was once nominated for a Nobel Peace Prize and which has strong links with the UN, attracts around 120,000 people to the main showground. And while for one week at least, the hills here are alive with the sound of music. For the rest of the year, it's walkers who flock to the area.

Two excellent long-range walks – the Dee Valley Way and the North Berwyn Way – meet in the town, while if you follow the canal path, it will

eventually take you over Thomas Telford's famous aqueduct. And while our route lies a few miles north of Pontcysyllte, if you are in the area then you would be foolish to miss it.

Standing 126 feet above the River Dee, it's an impressive piece of engineering, running nearly 200 feet across the valley. It's only 11 feet wide, while the canal itself is just 5 foot 3 inches deep. It's open to the public and you can walk across it fairly quickly, although with just one handrail running along the pedestrian side of the aqueduct it can feel a little hairy. Do the trip in a barge and you'll feel like you're floating through the sky – a bizarre experience.

The Llangollen end of the canal forms the first mile or so of this walk. It's a circular history trail packed with spectacular scenery with a real payoff at its climax in Dinas Brân castle, an atmospheric ruin at the very end of the walk with incredible views.

There is a straight two-mile vertical route up to the castle from the centre of the town but we don't want you to take that unless you're really stuck for time (or short on leg power!). Our preferred route is a slow, meandering ramble through this rich and rewarding part of Wales that's packed with stories and heritage. It's also very easy to find and follow. In fact of all the walks we've done in the Weatherman series, this has the easiest start point, as it kicks off from the famous stone arched bridge at the centre of the town.

Originally built in 1345 by John Trevor, the Bishop of St Asaph, it was the first stone structure to span the River Dee and was listed as one of the seven wonders of Wales in the famous poem:

Pistyll Rhaedr and Wrexham steeple,

Snowdon's mountain without its people,

Overton yew trees, St Winnifred's wells,

Llangollen bridge and Gresford bells.

Rebuilt in Elizabethan times, it remains unaltered on the lower side of the river, with the upper side being a perfectly copied reconstruction

from the 1870s. The square arch meanwhile was added to accommodate the railway station that runs alongside it and which went into service in 1862. The line carried passengers for over 100 years before closing in 1965 although a group of enthusiasts began to reclaim the track in the early 1970s, repairing the line and turning the station into a tourist attraction. These days they run their beautifully restored engines and carriages along seven and a half miles of track, to the delight of visitors and steam enthusiasts. As for the station, decked out like a period film set, it has a real timewarp factor and is well worth a visit before you set off.

Even if you don't take this delightful detour you'll be aware of the busy little station as you make your way around the route. That's because the shrill, piercing blast of the steam train whistles carry right across the mountains – although once you're on the path, you'll never actually spot the trains (apart from the odd smoky trail rising above the tree line as the engines puff past).

From the bridge you head up to the town's canal wharf, taking a left turn along the leafy tow path. It's as easy as walking gets, and if you aren't up to a rigorous workout, this first mile and a half or so is for you. The canal is one of the most scenic in the country and has even attracted the odd Hollywood A-lister to it (Harrison Ford – Indiana Jones – was spotted taking a barge holiday here some years ago).

Built by Thomas Telford, the canal was opened in 1805 and was intended to carry slate from the nearby quarries in the Horseshoe Pass. It was part of the Shropshire Union Canal system. At one time developers had planned to use it to link the Severn, the Dee and the Mersey rivers into one massive transport and trade route (an ambitious plan that never came to fruition).

Nowadays, the waterway is busy ferrying tourists up and down the canal and as you walk along you'll finds your progress shadowed by a small flotilla of barges and boats. As some of those barges are horsedrawn, you may want to watch where you step, too!

The canal path takes you above the famous Eisteddfod pavilion, and past the old chain bridge which still more or less spans the Dee. The canal runs out at the pumping station that feeds the waterway. From here you pass through a gate and into a sheep-filled field overlooking Telford's crescent-shaped weir. The weir provides you with the walk's first 'Kodak moment'. The path allows you to look down onto the perfect semi-circle of crystal clear water that rains off the razor-sharp edge in an artful waterfall.

At first, it's a bit odd to see the precisely-engineered architecture of the falls set against the natural river bank and meadow – there's an odd clash to the two styles that takes a moment or so to match up. But as you sit back on the high banking and take in the scene below you – usually accessorised with a fisherman or two – with the sound of the steam trains whistling in the distance and with a few sheep grazing the slopes, you'll soon appreciate that this is one of those special little places that make walking in Wales a real treat.

From here you head up to Llantysilio Church which is dedicated to St Tysilio, the son of a local prince called Ysgythrog, who lived around 500–580 AD. The current building was erected in 1180, although over the centuries it has been much improved upon and repaired. In fact much of what you can see today is actually Victorian reconstruction. The church grounds are a dedicated nature conservation area – meaning that the grass and vegetation is rarely cut during the year, allowing birds and wildlife to claim it and roam free. The broken gravestones, shadowed by ferns and covered in moss and ivy, create a suitably Gothic atmosphere, although it's more charming than chilling, and it's worth a quick detour to dawdle through the grounds.

The church itself is worth a look too. A plaque on the wall near the pulpit is dedicated to the poet Robert Browning who worshipped at Llantysilio for ten weeks during the autumn of 1886 (he was staying in the area visiting his friend Sir Theodore Martin, the biographer of Albert, the Prince Consort). There's also a narrow stained-glass window which dates from around 1460, and is believed to have originally hung in Valle Crucis Abbey – which we visit later on in the walk. The west window, meanwhile, is a great example of Pre-Raphaelite design.

Leaving the church through the wooden top gates, you turn right and keep on the main road until you hit a sign for Velvet Hill. Although these days it's overgrown with ferns and trees, it used to be heavily grazed, with sheep munching the grass down to the level of the moss growing through underneath, creating a soft 'velvet-like' landscape – hence the name. The hill also gives you your first proper view of the final destination, Dinas Brân Castle, which you'll see just as soon as the trail rises above the tree line and into a clearing.

The Welsh name for the hill is Coed Hirddyn which means 'wood of the long man' and may refer to the tall skeleton unearthed by archaeologists beneath Eliseg's Pillar – possibly the rudest monument in Wales. The pillar is all that remains of a huge stone cross near the foot of nearby Velvet Hill, which was erected here back in the 9th century and commemorates the life of an early ruler of Powys. Unfortunately following the English Civil War, Cromwell's followers decided that the cross was offensive. Which is ironic, if you look at what's left of it today – but more of that later.

Some more extravagant estimates had put the cross's original height at six metres, but all that remains now is a shaft of rock about two metres high. The Pillar gets its name from an inscription that was once visible on the stone, but which has long since weathered away. It told how Cyngen, the last king of Powys, had dedicated it to his great grandfather, King Eliseg, who had taken Powys from the English by force of arms.

The inscription on the rock today recalls how, in the 18th century, it was discovered lying in a field in a sorry state, before being re-erected. It's stood here ever since, although to some observers the column resembles a giant stone phallus! It certainly doesn't look like something which would tally with the Puritan aesthetic of Cromwell's followers. Back in the time of the Cistercian monks, however, it was still topped with a cross and the monument gave its name to the valley, and to the abbey that the monks would establish here in 1201.

You'll get a great view of the abbey as the path slopes down Velvet Hill, back to the main road (and if you turn left here and follow the road for about half a mile, you'll see the pillar in all its glory). It was home to 60 or so monks – around 20 'elite' choir monks and 40 lay brethren. The choir monks dedicated themselves to prayer and contemplation, while the lay brethren concentrated on more mundane tasks, like the agricultural work which allowed the community, in its early years, to be totally self-sufficient.

While Tintern Abbey is regarded as Wales' richest abbey, Valle Crucis was arguably just as well-off – probably more so. But because the monks deliberately under-declared their land and assets, they were never rated as highly as they should have been.

The abbey survived several attacks from the likes of Edward I and Owain Glyndŵr, as well as emerging from the ravages of the Black Death before it finally succumbed to the Dissolution in 1537. In the 16th century, the Eastern Range was converted into a house and a new roof line was

added, although that too had disappeared by the early 18th century. The ruins are equal to Tintern (if a little smaller) and it makes for a great way-stop before the real uphill climbs start on this walk. If you've got time to wander through the abbey, don't forget to check out the medieval fish pond at the back – it's the only remaining one in Wales, and it's a good spot to lie back and admire the architecture, picnic, and feed the ducks.

From the abbey, you walk through the neighbouring caravan park, over a wooden bridge across the river, and then head up – first through farmland, and then through forest, as the walk winds its long way to the foot of Dinas Brân hill. On the way you should get some great views of the Berwyn Hills (there's a handy seated stop along the way so you can soak up the scenery in comfort).

As you slog up towards the castle look out for a big carved crow that marks the way. Dinas Brân translates as 'the Crow's Fortress' and you should see the birds flying overhead as you climb the path. The castle is a place of myth and legend. The Holy Grail was supposed to have been kept on the site back in the first century while other tales tell of evil spirits haunting the place, of hidden treasure in the hills and of the giant Geomagog who supposedly established an early stronghold here.

The ruined castle was built on the remains of a prehistoric earthwork that is still visible on the eastern ridge of the hill. It's an obvious place for a fortress. The hill dominates the landscape and stands at over 1,000 feet (305 metres) above sea level, while the sides of the northern slope form a natural fortification so steep that the medieval moat and outer wall only needed to extend around the southern and eastern sides.

Dinas Brân was probably built by Prince Gruffudd ap Madoc in the early 1260s, at the same time as his ally, Prince Llywelyn of Gwynedd, was raising similar fortresses to secure his lands. In fact, Llywelyn's hilltop fort at Dolforwyn, near Newtown, is very similar in design and execution, and may have been crafted by the same master mason.

Despite its present-day appearance, Dinas Brân would have been a castle that impressed visitors not just with its strength, but with its splendour and intricate craftsmanship. So who is to blame for the windswept ruins? Well, when war broke out between Llywelyn and Edward I in 1276, the fate of the castle, which had passed to Madoc's sons, became bound in a bitter family feud.

The two eldest brothers made their peace with the English, leaving Owain and Gruffudd (the two younger brothers who still had control of Dinas Brân) to take desperate measures. With the English troops camped below them under the command of the Earl of Lincoln, the Welsh seemed convinced that despite the advantage of geography, they would be unable to successfully defend the fort. As they could not let such a formidable stronghold fall into enemy hands, they decided to set it on fire. And that was that.

Even though Lincoln advised Edward that the fire had not completely damaged the fort and that no castle in Wales or England was stronger or harder to attack, Dinas Brân was never fully repaired and was allowed to fall into ruin.

But by the 18th century, these evocative remains were attracting a different type of English visitor, as Dinas Brân became an early tourist destination. Wordsworth was one of many who came here (he had probably wandered in, lonely as a cloud), and was moved to write about Brân's 'shattered galleries and roofless halls'. In Victorian times the site was so popular that entrepreneurs installed a camera obscura at the top and a small tea kiosk (fed daily by a tea lady who used a donkey to bring supplies up the hill). It's still a popular attraction now, as is the whole of this history trail which attracts around 50,000 walkers a year.

Those that brave the climb are rewarded with a fantastic panoramic view over Llangollen that takes in the town, the moorland-clad ridge of Llantysilio Mountain, the Berwyns and the cliff-like scarp of Eglwyseg – an impressive and geologically important rock face to the north. There are also equally impressive views of the Dee Valley, the Shropshire Plain and the viaduct that carries the railway to Ruabon, while further east you'll see the canal and that famous aqueduct. From here, a grateful walker will be relieved to learn that the

path is all downhill and within twenty minutes or so you can be back on that bridge in the centre of town.

From Victorian ingenuity to Cistercian tranquillity, from medieval warfare to tales of myth and legend, this route is a real time-traveller, with enough variety in landscape and attractions to keep anyone happy. It's also easily broken down into smaller foot-friendly chunks for those who aren't up to the full walk but want an easygoing and really rewarding ramble through this fantastic part of Wales.

The Sugar Loaf

Near: Abergavenny

Ordnance Survey Grid Reference SH 862941

OS Explorer Map 215

Derek says…

There are a few ways up Sugar Loaf Mountain; this route is a quiet and peaceful option. The walk begins and ends in historical Abergavenny, but much of the walk is in the countryside, passing an underground reservoir and ancient woods along the way.

I really enjoyed ambling through the beautiful St Mary's Vale – especially in spring when the bluebells are out – although it can get muddy after heavy rain, when the Nant Iago stream can turn into a watery torrent!

It's a fair hike up Sugar Loaf Mountain, or Mynydd Pen-y-Fal in Welsh, which is the highest point in the area at 598 metres (1,962 ft). From the top you can see the Bristol Channel and the Brecon Beacons in good weather, but wear something warm because it is exposed on the summit.

As you head back down, pop into the Sugar Loaf Vineyard. Here you can sample some fine local wine and enjoy panoramic views of the Usk Valley. If you're feeling fit, how about taking part in the Three Peaks Walk which is organised every March? This involves climbing the Blorenge, the Sugar Loaf and the Skirrid all in one day! I'm worn out just thinking about it!

The many lovely features of this area make this walk interesting and invigorating. If you don't fancy following the crowds up Sugarloaf Mountain, why not take your time meandering along the beech-lined Nant Iago in St Mary's Vale before ambling to the vineyard to sample their fine wines? If you start to feel footsore you can always dabble your toes in a crisp mountain stream or paddle in the velvety waters of the River Usk.

Of all the walks I love, the one through St Mary's Vale always evokes happy childhood memories of berry picking, summer picnics, dappled green shade and young lads tickling for trout. I hope it leaves you with that same feeling of lazy contentment at the end of the day (especially if you have a glass or two of Sugarloaf wine to hand!).

Fiona Ford

Torfaen Borough Council

97

The sign at the entrance to Abergavenny tells you that this is 'the Gateway to Wales' and for many walkers heading down the M4 corridor, the town is the first port of call for a weekend out on the hills. The great attraction of the place (apart from the fact that it's one of the country's busier and prettier market towns) is that it's surrounded by lots of easily accessible walking country.

It's (just about) ringed by two mountains and five hills, the three most famous being the Blorenge mountain, Skirrid Fawr (both of which were covered in the last book) and – the biggest and best – the Sugar Loaf mountain (or Pen y Fal as it's known in Welsh). Oh, and if you're interested, the other four hills are the Deri, the Skirrid Fach, the Rholben and Mynydd Llanwenarth – and yes, they're all worth a walk too!

But it's the Sugar Loaf that is the big daddy of Abergavenny routes. This volcano-shaped peak lords it over the surrounding area and is a fairly straightforward walk, with a steady climb and gorgeous views over the Usk Valley, the Beacons and the Black Mountains. It's a classic summer walk, beloved of local families and if you fancy a quick up-and-down amble to the thin ridge of the Loaf's flat top, then you can drive to within an hour of the summit and leave the car at a handy and busy little car park. Do that, and you could be up and down in two hours.

Of course, we're not going to suggest that you do that – as ever, we have a greater ambition for this walk. Because if you're not a local, then the Sugar Loaf is the ideal carrot to encourage you to take a much longer walk that will give you a taste of the town itself. Put simply, the summit isn't the whole story with this walk. Because while it gives you a real sense of achievement to make it to the top, this route offers lots more, in terms of intrigue, history and some interesting diversions.

Abergavenny gets its name from the Brythonic word *gobannia*, meaning 'river of blacksmiths' and it relates to the town's early importance in iron smelting. The river later became Gafenni in Welsh, and so Abergavenny (obviously) means 'mouth of the river Gafenni'. There was also a Roman garrison here once, called Gobannium. It's long gone now of course, and its remains were only discovered relatively recently, when the foundations for the town's new post office building were dug back in the 1960s. It was part of a network linked to the bigger Roman forts at Usk and Caerleon, and the troops there were largely employed in keeping the local Silure tribes in line.

Historically speaking, if you were looking for trouble – then this was the right place to come to. Abergavenny lies within 10 miles of the English border, and as such the town has a long history of conflict that runs from the Romans right up until the Civil War. It's much quieter these days, however. And if you're a walker, you're spoilt for choice here. As well as all the smaller local paths, the Offa's Dyke walk passes near here, while the Marches Way, Beacons Way and the Usk Valley Walk all run through the town centre.

Our walk is a circular route, which starts at the town's Castle Meadows car park near Linda Vista gardens and in the shadow of Abergavenny Castle. The castle was built by the Norman lord Hamelin de Balloon in 1087 and was destroyed in 1233 by the Earl of Pembroke and the Welsh princes. Before that, the old timber Great Hall was famously the scene of a massacre, when the Norman Baron of Abergavenny William de Braose lured various local chieftains there on Christmas day in 1175. Having arrived under a truce they left their weapons at the door and, once inside, were ambushed and butchered when de Braose sprung his trap.

The walls you see today are the remains of a stone hall built between 1233 and 1295. The Tower complex dates to around 1300 while the Gate House was remodelled right up until the early 15th century. Try and find the time to look around the castle. If you do, just take into account that the pristine Keep (which houses the town's museum) was built in 1818 as a hunting lodge for the Marquess of Abergavenny (the original was destroyed around 1645).

From the car park you head up toward the town's police station. As you do that you'll pass Linda Vista gardens on your left hand side. These are public gardens, laid out in the grounds of a former gentleman's residence

and again are worth a visit at either end of the trip. If you do decide to drop in, look out for their rather fine collection of trees, and try and find a carved wooden totem pole sculpture, which depicts the Christmas Day massacre as well as an attack on the town by Owain Glyndŵr.

Once on the main road, cross over and take a look at some tall, three-storey red brick terraced houses. In the middle of the two twinned homes, you'll see a date laid out in brick (1910) and an ornate letter 'A' above it. This is the insignia of the Marquis of Abergavenny. He also used the sign of a portcullis gate and a bull's head too, and you'll spot more of these crests on the next row of houses you encounter when you turn right into Pant Lane.

From this slight hill, you'll also get the first glimpse of the mountain you're about to climb. But that climb is a long way off yet, and there's still more of the town to take in. So from here you drop down near the main road, passing the Station Hotel away to your far right. This used to be the site of the town's second railway station (the other is still in use today, on the other side of the town) and was once home to one of the largest rail sidings in Wales. This line connected the town to Tredegar and Merthyr Tydfil (via Brynmawr) with the branch line being opened in 1862. That second station and line was in service until 1958, although nothing much survives of it now apart from the odd pub name and the terraced cottages built to house the workers.

You'll pass those as you head into Stanhope Street (via Chapel Road). From here you'll encounter a leafier, more suburban landscape as you turn into Avenue Road and walk the boundary of the local cricket club (a sometime venue for the Glamorgan County Cricket side).

Having dabbled in the town's railway and Norman history, the next section gives a taste of the ecclesiastical heritage of Abergavenny. Leaving the cricket ground you pass through an avenue of Horse Chestnut trees and Lime (or Linden) trees. You also get a good view of the Deri – easily identifiable because, like a monk's haircut, it wears a band of trees as a collar to its bare-headed hill. The Deri was also the source of the red sandstone that those earlier terraced cottages were made from.

At the top of Avenue Road you'll enter a private lane where you'll spot a large barn-shaped building which has been absorbed into a large house. Parts of the barn used to belong to the old chapel of St David's, an outpost of the main priory back in the centre of the town. A former chapel of ease, it was abandoned and then reclaimed as part of the barn back in the 15th century.

From here you head through a kissing gate and then turn right onto Chain Lane, which comes with a great view of the Blorenge mountain (to your left). You then go uphill past the lodge house of Llwyn Du Court, along a sunken country lane. This is part of the ancient manor of Llwyn Du (the Black Grove) owned by the Priory until the dissolution of the monastries, when it passed to the Lordship of Abergavenny.

From here, you've walked beyond the town and begin heading slowly towards the Sugar Loaf. As you begin to climb, look out for a big green mound on your right. It's not the Teletubbies' hill, but an underground reservoir, built to replace the old open reservoir at Pen y Pound, following rumours that a dead donkey had been found floating in it! Ahead of you lies St David's Vale, or Deer Park as it's known locally. This was a valley that was walled in medieval times, and which supplied the monks with venison (hence the name the Deer Park). The deer park covered over 500 acres, and if you look at the OS map, you can still see the line of the old enclosure.

From here you head up onto another of those Abergavenny hills – the Rholben. This is where the hill starts to bite as you follow a track to your right that takes you up the brow of the hill, and to your first full view

of the Sugar Loaf proper. From here, the way ahead is fairly straightforward – you just go up! There are a number of routes to the top and this one has the advantage of taking you through the woodland on your way up.

The slopes of the Sugar Loaf are heavy with bracken and whinberries – and more often than not – lots of walkers. On a sunny Sunday afternoon this can be a very popular destination – which is why we chose our 'town trail', because at least this way you're guaranteed some valuable peace and quiet and a bit more 'bang' for your walking 'buck'. Because once you hit the approach to the narrow table top of the mountain, this walk is all about the sky above your head, the fresh air, the sumptuous views and the satisfaction of reaching the peak. So just pick a path through the undergrowth – there are various criss-crossing tracks – and get moving.

You can quickly get a suntan up here, even on a breezy autumn walk. So on a hot August day, take care that you don't end up with a red neck or a scorched set of ears, as there's no cover, and with your eyes fixed on the ground rising ahead of you, you can burn without realising it. Every 100 yards or so of ascent reveals a little more of the town below and the hills beyond, but if you can hold back from looking until the summit, the final payoff will come as a genuinely pleasant surprise.

The final 30 yards of the mountain is a steep semi-scramble that will remind your thighs and knees that this is a mountain and not a hill, and then you're at the top. The summit is about 100 metres long with a collection of crags and rocky outcrops at both the eastern and western ends. From the trig point you'll see the Black Mountains to the north, the Brecon Beacons to the west, the Blorenge and both Skirrids to the south, plus the Forest of Dean stretching away to the east. On a clear day you'll also see the Severn and the Bristol Channel glittering away in the distance to the south.

It's a perfect place to raid your rucksack and feast before heading back down towards the town over the other side of the Rholben and then along the scenic path through St Mary's Vale. As you wander down through the woods you cross an old Clapper-style stone bridge near a ford over the Nant Iago (or the James stream). It's another good reason to do this walk in the summer, as the river can rise here in winter, leaving you to splash through this footpath in ankle-high water.

Eventually the track gets firmer and takes you out of the trees, at which point you get a great view of the Usk and of Nevill Hall Hospital below. The hospital is a typical tiered and drab 1960s concrete block, although it's set in the beautiful formal grounds of the ornate Victorian house beyond the main hospital building. This was Neville Hall and it belonged to a former Marquise of Abergavenny – the same man whose crest can be seen on so many of the houses in the town.

Turn left here from the track and head down the lane, where you're in for a pleasant surprise as you find yourself beside the slopes of a vineyard. The Sugar Loaf Vineyard harvests around five acres of grapes each year for a range of locally-produced wine. They grow red and white grapes (two acres of the former and three of the latter) which produce anywhere between 6,000 to 15,000 bottles a year. They also encourage people to drop in to the visitor centre and to take a walk around the vineyards. They'll also let you sample the wines, so this might make for a good rest point after your descent – although it could prove costly, as Derek left with a bottle or two in his rucksack!

From the vineyard you cross the road, head over a stile and walk down past Pentre House, a former farmhouse which was extensively remodelled in the early 1800s, and which has a small herd of hairy Highland Cattle that roam the surrounding parkland. The house is famous for a notorious robbery back at the beginning of the 19th century when the family silver was taken in a daring raid that shocked the sleepy town. Further shocks came when the said silver turned up in the Bluebell Inn in Tudor Street, Abergavenny. Following its discovery, the landlord was convicted of theft and transported to Australia as punishment.

Speaking of landlords, you pass alongside the Lamb and Flag pub as you continue your walk back down into town (so coupled with the vineyard, this could be a walk worth working up a thirst for). Cross the main road here, then take a right turn over another stile at the side of some outbuildings. From here you walk across some fields and then onto the lane that passes the former garden of the old village school, before arriving at the church of St Peters in Llanwenarth Citra.

Llanwenarth is split into upper and lower halves (Ultra and Citra) by the river. The Ultra part of the parish covers the area of Govilon whilst Citra stretches from the river to the top of the Sugar Loaf. The two sides used to be connected by a rope-pulled ferry which, every Sunday, would transport parishioners from either half of the village across the water to their relevant churches. For example, from the Citra side, people crossed to visit the Govoilon Baptist Chapel (which, coincidently, is the oldest Baptist chapel in Wales) while those belonging to the Church of England had to go from the Ultra side to St Peter's, until they finally had their own church built in 1848.

St Peter's has probably been a religious site since pre-Christian times and it was a solid choice for a place of worship, because when the River Usk floods, it often leaves the church high and dry, cut-off (but crucially safe) and stranded in a sea of brown water. The church was refashioned by the Victorians but some of its old character remains and you can find a stone font inside that dates back to Saxon times.

From the church we turn right and then immediately cross over a stile into fields. These lead to the river bank and the site of the old ferry is to your left. Those of you with an interest in political scandal might also be interested to learn that the white cottage opposite is known as Ferry Cottage, and was allegedly a hiding place for Christine Keeler, following the Profumo Affair.

From here you turn left and follow the river bank back to Abergavenny.

About a mile before you hit the town though you pass the sad site of Steel's Memorial, which was built to commemorate the son of a local doctor who drowned at this point of the river back in the latter half of the 19th century. Ironically the memorial itself is now submerged in the water due to the river eroding the bank, and only the railings around it are left above water – although if you're lucky you'll be able to spot the stone itself if you peer over the side into the river below.

You'll now be close to Llanfoist bridge, but before you step up to it, look closely at the river bed and you should be able to see the round indentations of the big iron pillars that once supported the railway line to Merthyr.

The bridge itself is actually two bridges spliced together – and you can appreciate the join if you look up at the arches. You should see that they don't match up and that the arches don't meet squarely in the middle. Originally the bridge was a narrow medieval construction that dates back to the late 12th century. This is the bridge on the town side. In 1814 it was joined by a new bridge that carried a horse-drawn tram across the Usk, and which was used to ferry goods and materials from Blaenavon and Govoilon Wharf to Hereford. When the railway came to town, the tram was rendered obsolete, but instead of being demolished, the bridge was reduced in height and joined onto the old medieval bridge that ran alongside it, thus widening the access for road traffic.

Get beyond the bridge and you'll find yourself in Castle Meadows and almost in sight of the end of the walk. As the name suggests, this is a wide stretch of public access land, that runs alongside the river with the castle standing guard above it. Beloved of dog walkers (and the anglers who relax on the banks here while fishing in the Usk), it's a flat, friendly final leg that takes you over a stile and back into the car park.

If you've paced yourself then you should have ample opportunity to explore the Linda Vista Gardens or the castle.

And if you do find yourself wanting even more of a challenge, then maybe you should consider the Abergavenny Three Peaks challenge. The brainchild of local walking guru (and sometime Weatherman Walking guide) Chris Barber, this is a boot-busting route that adds the Skirrid and the Blorenge to a trail that clocks in at around 20 miles (and which includes 5,000 metres of ascent). It was first run in 1963 and is held annually under the auspices of the Cardiff Outdoor Group – if you're interested, then Google the challenge, and check out the official website.

Conversely, if our route looks a bit daunting, then remember you can take this trail apart and do it in sections: the town trail, the Sugar Loaf itself, and the walk along the Usk are each engrossing enough in their own right to keep you fit and interested. That's the beauty of walking – you choose your pace, your goals and your destination. And if your choice for a lengthy stroll is the Sugar Loaf, then we'll bet that you won't be disappointed.

Gower

Near: Swansea

Ordnance Survey Grid Reference SH 862941

OS Explorer Map 215

The Gower Peninsula is a beautiful part of Wales, and this walk has something for everyone: a wonderful beach, stunning views and an old cast-iron lighthouse at Whiteford Sands.

The walk starts at Rhossili, a pretty village with a lovely church. Take care if you're planning to walk over to Worm's Head. Many people have been caught out – including Dylan Thomas – so remember to check the tide times.

This is also a great spot for birdwatching, with an abundance of seabirds including razorbills, guillemots, fulmars, puffins and oystercatchers, so make sure you bring your binoculars. The walk up to Rhossili Down may leave you out of breath, but the views from the top are magnificent. When the visibility is good, you can see for miles along the coast and the sunsets can be spectacular.

The one thing you notice on this walk is how exposed you are to the elements. Being so close to the sea, there isn't much protection from the sun and the wind, so hold onto your hat and remember the sun cream! By the way, if you haven't got a car, you can always hop on and off the Gower Explorer bus which stops at various places on the peninsula.

This walk takes you across the width of Gower, from the dramatic tidal island of Worm's Head to the iconic Victorian cast-iron lighthouse at Whiteford Point. You will enjoy stunning coastal scenery, wildlife, archaeology and beautiful commons landscapes. Rhossili Down, Hardings Down and Llanmadoc Hill are all worth climbing for the spectacular views across inland Gower and out to the changing seascapes of Bristol Channel to the south and Burry Inlet to the north.

The flora and fauna includes seabirds and seals breeding on Worm's Head National Nature Reserve (NNR), spectacular heath land and spiralling skylarks across the commons, and dunes carpeted in wild flowers at Whiteford NNR. The archaeology is also impressive: Neolithic burial chambers, Bronze Age cairns, Iron Age hill forts and the remains of a WWII firing range and radar station.

It is the sheer variety packed into a small peninsula that makes Gower such a special place.

Sian Musgrave
Head Warden,
National Trust
Wales

Sion Brackenbury
Gower Commons Initiative

Start

If you've ever been to the Gower then you can probably skip this chapter because you won't need any encouragement from us to visit it. And if you've never been to the Gower – then frankly – why the hell not?

Seriously, it's one of the most beautiful places in Britain, a gorgeous peninsula beloved of beach bums, surfers, sun lovers, walkers and other groups of laid back fun-seekers who know that when all is said and done, life is a beach. And this route, which celebrates the beauty and bountiful charms of Rhossili, gives you plenty of opportunity to get sand in your shoes. It also takes you to an awe-inspiring ruin of a lighthouse and lets you run wild above the jaws of a sea dragon. Throw in a couple of Iron Age forts, a church with a connection to Scott's doomed Antarctic expedition and tales of shipwrecks (and shipwreckers) and you've a monster of a walk.

It clocks in at nearly ten miles and it benefits from a degree of forward planning. For a start, the route is peppered with bus stops for the excellent Gower Explorer service (and there's a stop at – just about – either end of the walk) so you have the option of taking a breather and breaking up the trip with some eco-friendly travel. Even if you cheat though, this walk will present you with some difficult choices if you want to include all of the sights and destinations that we hit on the television show. The reason is the tides.

You see, the walk starts and ends in two unique and spectacular

locations, but both are only accessible at a low tide. And the chances of you making both and beating the sea are pretty much impossible. So if you want the best of both worlds, time to soak up the sights at your leisure and a stress-free ramble, then split this walk up. Either ditch the Worm's Head section (leaving that treat for another day) and instead time your trip around the tides at Whiteford, or, split the walk in half and make the Bulwark Fort at Llanmadoc the place for the break. At least that way you're guaranteed not to miss a thing. After all, tides wait for no man. Not even Dylan Thomas, the local literary icon who came a cropper when visiting Worm's Head as a boy (but more of that later).

Given that the sea will control much of what happens on land with this walk, you need to get good up-to-the-minute information before you start off. That's not a problem here.

We started our walk in the car park behind the National Trust Visitor centre at Rhossili. In many ways this is a dangerous place for walkers, because the view of the beach from here can prove too tempting. You could find yourself ditching the rucksack for a bucket and spade and surrendering to the beautiful bay below. Not many would blame you, either, if you were swayed by the golden sands. Rhossili is the most westerly bay on the Gower and the beach here stretches for three miles, with the north end at Llangennith a Mecca for local surfers.

The walk gives you unparalleled views of this unspoilt perfect beach, particularly as you leave Rhossili and climb the downs. But before you head for the high ground to take in that panorama, we recommend you do a bit of exploring first. That's why we head left from the visitor centre, down the main drag towards Worm's Head.

It's a fantastically evocative name for a really special – and at times strange and magical – place. It gets its name from the old Norse word for dragon ('wurme') because to the Viking visitors to Gower, the jagged rocky outcrop looked for all the world like the snout and maw of a great fossilised lizard, with the neck and head sliding lazily into the mist and spray of the Irish Sea.

And while it may have looked fierce to the raiders in their longboats, up close it can cause a few worries for pedestrians too. Make no mistake it can be a treacherous place to get to, linked to the mainland by a tidal causeway with no clear path from shore to shore. So before you set off, a word of caution. The rocks can be slippery and the tides can come in fast; that's why you should take the time to call in to Coastwatch control centre.

Housed in the old Victorian coastguard hut overlooking the causeway and manned by volunteers, this is the place to get all your information about tide times and weather. They'll also advise you on whether you're equipped for the journey and will call out the coastguard if you get into trouble. After checking your times and working out how long you have to get on and off and explore the Head, you take a zig-zag path down to the rocks.

Picking your way over the mussel shells, rock pools and the flotsam and jetsom, you eventually clamber on to the Worm where you are faced with a short, sharp shock of a vertical climb. Once over that obstacle you find yourself on the flat-topped Inner Head of the dragon, looking towards the Outer Head and the sea beyond. The Worm is about a mile long and about 100 yards across at its widest point (reaching 150 feet at its highest point). From the Inner Head, you cross the natural rock arch of the Devil's Bridge, before mounting the Low Neck and then hitting the Outer Head.

The Outer Head is a breeding ground for seabirds like herring gulls, guillemots, razorbills and kittiwakes. You'll occasionally see a puffin or two put in appearance as well!. Walkers are requested not to approach the Outer Head between March 1 and August 31st though as this interferes with the birds' breeding season. So a September slot for this route is just right. The Outer Head is also home to the Worm's Head cave and on the north side, a blow hole, which adds to the dragon's character, as it makes a noise which is an odd mixture of booming sea roll and hissing spray – so it sounds like the beast is breathing (or snoring!).

The soil on the Worm is particularly fertile, and in the past, sheep farmers used it as rich grazing ground (mutton from the Worm was supposed to taste better than that from any other part of the Gower). These days, the land is protected as a National Nature Reserve and, as ungrazed grassland, boasts a wide variety of plant species. But remember if you wanted to take the time to track them down, the Worm crossing is only exposed for two and a half hours every day before and after low tide. The Coastguard Bell at the top of the causeway isn't there for decoration, and it's easy to get caught out.

Even Dylan Thomas made the mistake, falling asleep on the island as a young man, and waking to find himself stranded there with nothing but a bag of sandwiches and a good book to keep him company. He wrote about the experience later, recalling how he sat on the hill of the Worm from dusk to midnight, cold and frightened, waiting for the tips of the reef to reappear before he could venture back to the shore. Hopefully you'll do the trip without any similar drams!

On the way back over, try and look out for a huge rusting anchor set

into the sand. It belongs to a cargo boat called the Samuel which was carrying 500 tons of coal from Swansea when it ran aground in November 1884. The local lifeboat rescued the crew while the coal was sold to local farmers (who in turn sold it to other locals – keeping the village of Rhossili in cheap fuel for years).

You'll pass the remains of another wreck as you head back past the beach, but before you catch sight of that, there are two much earlier historical sites to look out for. Both are quite hard to spot from ground level. The first is an intricate medieval field system called the Vile, a local name for the cultivated strips of land that spread across the headland to Mewslade Bay. The Vile is still farmed in a traditional way and has a dry stone wall boundary constructed with an overhang to stop sheep from leaping over into the fields. This style of wall is special to the Gower and building it is something of a lost art.

The Vile lies to the right of the path while on the left, clinging to the cliffside is the Old Castle. This is the first of three Iron Age forts you'll encounter on this walk, and is not only the smallest, but the hardest to spot as bracken and gorse obscure the bumps and lumps of the garrison's remains. It's all evidence of the sheer length of time human beings have lived and worked here in Gower.

There is plenty of evidence of Mesolithic activity in the area, like the Foxhole cave where flint tools and other materials were uncovered, while the Paviland cave is just down the coast from here, home to the famous

Red Lady of Paviland.

Paviland is one of the most important prehistoric sites in Britain. It was here that the remains of an Upper Palaeolithic burial site were discovered back in 1823 by the Rev. William Buckland. Because he was a Creationist and believed that no human remains could pre-date the Great Flood, he wildly underestimated the age of his find. Coupled with the fact that the bones were dyed red (they had been stained with ochre), the small size of the body (which was dressed with ivory necklaces) led him to guess that this was the grave of a Roman witch or prostitute. Later tests revealed the skeleton to be that of a man (probably that of a tribal chief, hence the jewellery) and was dated back as far as around 28,000 BC.

The next historical site that you will encounter on the walk is a lot younger than that. As you head back towards the Visitor Centre, peer down onto the beach below and, if the tide is with you, you should be able to spot some strange dark shapes jutting out of the sand. The black and rotten stumps and planks are all that remains of the Helvetia. This was a Norwegian vessel that ran aground here in October 1887. On this occasion, it was a cargo of timber that the residents of Rhossili were able to help themselves to, before the authorities collected what was left and sold it at auction.

The path now takes you through the village and up to the Down but before you head for the hills, if you have time, stop off at St Mary's Church. Inside is a memorial to Petty Officer Edgar Evans, born in Rhossili in 1876, and a key member of Captain Scott's doomed expedition to the South Pole. Evans was baptised in the church, and even married here in 1904.

However, a taste for adventure continually led the explorer far from home and eventually saw him sign up for the ill-fated mission. He was the first of the team to die, passing away on February 17, 1917 after falling and injuring himself on the Beardsmore Glacier some days earlier.

The entrance to the church is also worth a look. The stone archway surrounding the door pre-dates the 13th-century structure and is believed to have been salvaged from the original church, which was destroyed in storms that covered it and most of the village in sand. The arch is Norman and beautifully carved, while the church also has a 'leper's window' on the south side of the building, a 14th-century addition that allowed sufferers from the disease to participate in mass and attend confession without having to go inside.

St Mary's is your last port of call in Rhossili. Once you leave the village, you turn left and climb onto the Down where you are rewarded with some amazing views of Worm's Head and the coast. It's also a good place to appreciate that celebrated medieval 'wrong-ness' of the Vile and the narrow finger strip field pattern. At this point of the walk, though, we kept the beach-gazing and photograph-taking to a minimum (hard as that was to do) and got down to some serious walking. As such, we spurned the chance to explore both the Sweyne's Howes burial chambers and the remains of a World War Two radar station, and instead headed inwards towards Hardings Down and the Gower Common.

This is another unique environment. The National Trust owns over 1,760 hectares of common on Gower; the local authority being the other significant land owner in the area. The common has been inhabited and farmed for thousands of years, as the two major Iron Age hill forts found here prove. It is still grazed today, by a collection of ponies, cattle and sheep, the mix of animals vital in preserving the unique common environment. All are owned by local 'commoners' who have the right to turn their livestock loose here. This traditional practice of letting the animals roam free to graze has created a rich tapestry of heath land, wetland and mire and is protected by European legislation as a Special

Area of Conservation. The ponies and cattle also help to fight the incursion of bracken, which would otherwise out-compete some of the more important plants like certain heathers and ericas, as well as grasses like the fescues and other slow-growing species.

All of these suffer in the low light conditions caused by the overshading of the bullying and overbearing bracken. The plant is also in danger of swamping the Iron Age forts, as you'll appreciate when you approach Hardings Down, a vast earthwork covering three sites and most of the hill. Partial excavations of the site have revealed that the fort had a cobbled entrance with grand, high wooden gates, while other remains suggested timber frame houses near the fort, as well as animal enclosures and other structures. The Commons Initiative, a body aimed at preserving the environment of the area does carry out annual bracken clearance, and following a cut, the fort is much easier to see and to navigate. However with fewer grazing animals on the common and a lack of penetrating frosts, the bracken is a formidable foe for farmer, archaeologist and environmentalist alike.

From Hardings Down you're treated to another set of outstanding views. You can see Burry Port to the north, Llanelli to the north-east, Exmoor to the south-east, and the Bristol Channel to the south. As you spin around to take it all in, you get a real sense of Gower as a peninsula with the sea on (almost!) all sides, and a host of bays and beautiful places to explore. From here you can also see the next fort on our journey, the Bulwark on Llanmadoc Hill.

Built, not quite in spear-throwing distance of its neighbour, but still close enough for a serious row, this is the most interesting of the Iron

Age garrisons, by virtue of the fact that its earthworks are more pronounced, and the ridges and mounds more defined. It has more of a sense of structure and again incredible views; this time out over Whiteford, Broughton Bay and the Pembrokeshire coastline. On a good day, you can spot Lundy Island off the Devon coast and Caldy Island off Tenby, while a look back down the coast towards the tip of Worm's Head will make you realise just how far you've come (and how far there is yet to go).

As for the Bulwark, as a fort, it has a more complex system of enclosures than its neighbour, with well-preserved and prominent banks and ditches. At 186 metres, the old red sandstone hill at Llanmadoc is one of the highest points on Gower, and one of the mysteries of the Bulwark is that the fort is not sited on the summit of the hill (as was the usual practice) but instead sits at an angle on the slope, looking towards Cheriton.

Legend has it that the chieftain of this sloping fort, Tonkin, was horribly murdered during a battle with the tribe from Hardings Down. This bloody skirmish was known as the battle of Tankey Lake Moor. No one knows who started it or who won, but we do know it wasn't pretty as the name translates into 'lake of blood', which refers to the aftermath of this particular local quarrel.

From here you head off the common and return briefly to the 21st century in the shape of Llanmadoc. A typical pretty Gower village (with a good walker's pub, the Britannia), it was named after the local church of St Madoc and is a handy place to catch your breath before the last leg of this epic trek! This is a real leg-stretcher of a walk through nature reserve, forest, salt marsh and beach. You reach it by passing through the small hamlet of Cwm Ivy (which has a handy car park at which you can arrange to be picked up, or just drive straight to if you're only interested in the Whiteford leg of the journey). There's also another Gower Explorer bus stop near here too.

This final section is a real Gower secret. The peninsula as a whole gets around 3 million visitors a year, yet this is one of those places that never attracts a crowd whatever the time of year or weather. Even people who regularly visit Gower and 'know' the area will quite probably be ignorant of Whiteford Sands and the beautiful countryside that surrounds it.

Gower was the UK's first designated Area of Outstanding Natural Beauty (it was awarded the honour in 1956 and is one of only five in Wales). And it's places like this which led to that award: a wonderful mixture of habitat, a Wales in miniature, lit with a pure natural glow and blessed with peace and quiet.

Llanrhidian, for example, has one of the best salt marsh habitats in Britain. The marsh spreads into this leg of the walk, and is of international importance for its enormous population of wintering wildfowl and waders, including oystercatchers, knot, pintail and golden plover. Meanwhile the dune system of Whiteford Burrows is home to many rare species of flower, including early marsh orchid, fen orchid, early grass and dune gentian.

A gate leads you away from Cwm Ivy and down into the Whiteford Burrows National Nature Reserve, which begins with a small forest of leggy pines. The evergreens extend as far as the dune system where you should run into the local wildlife – one of the many small packs of wild ponies who lazily patrol the area, picking at the rough grass. They have a confident swagger about them and provide real entertainment particularly when the tide comes in. Over time they have learned exactly where the tide crests the dunes and so pick out the easiest attainable high ground to keep their hooves dry from the sea.

As well as interrupting the ponies' grazing, the tide here occasionally

throws up a different kind of distraction: old army ordinance – bomb shells if you like – left over from the time when the estuary was part of a practice range. Most of the UXBs (unexploded bombs) came from the old firing range at Crofty, while some were dropped by aeroplane from RAF Fairwood Common. But don't panic, you are unlikely to stumble across any live ammunition or shells while you're out and about. And of course in the event that you do see something suspicious, then you're advised to leave it alone and contact the authorities. Besides, you have more important things to look at, because at the end of the beach (if you've timed your trip accordingly and the tide allows it) you will get to see one of Gower's most stunning landmarks in all its glory.

A 15-minute walk across the beach from the dunes will bring you to the foot of the spectacular Whiteford Lighthouse. Built in 1865, it dominates the flat, pewter landscape of the puddled, rocky shore like an elaborate black birdcage, standing huge, eerie and forbidding (especially if the black gulls and cormorants are roosting in its exposed upper reaches).

It's a brilliant example of design from the heyday of Victorian engineering. Considering its remote position, the attention to detail is simply staggering. It truly is a thing of beauty, elegantly crafted with porthole windows and a finial on the top. It was made of prefabricated cast iron sections and assembled slowly over time, piece by piece as the tide would allow. Although it has a room at the top, it was never lived in, and as such, this was probably a contingency plan in case the crew working at the lighthouse was caught out by the tide, and forced to sit it out until the sea receded.

Although it is abandoned and dilapidated now, it is the only waveswept cast-iron lighthouse in the UK – in fact there's only one other in the world, in Barbados. Not so long ago it was offered for sale for the price of £1. The catch? Prospective buyers had to prove they had £200,000 waiting to spend on renovating the structure. There were no takers.

Whiteford was used until 1921 when it was superseded by a new lighthouse further up the bay at Burry Holmes. These days it's an atmospheric and weird relic, something that seems just too bizarre a structure to be stranded in this beautiful but desolate stretch of the coast. It's a great way to finish the walk and a fitting bookend to the equally emotive Worm's Head which kicked us off nearly 10 miles earlier. It's also the reason we advise you think long and hard about how much time you need to do this walk justice.

To miss either showpiece because of the tide would be a real shame; that's why, if there's any doubt, you should be sensible, and plan to do the route over two days. After all, there are far worse places than Gower to visit more than once. And while you may think you know it, having hit the beaches once or twice, or maybe driven through it on a few occasions, this is a place which begs to be explored on two feet. And remember, both the lighthouse and Worm's Head are only accessible to walkers. They are ours and ours alone.

Pontypool

Near: Pontypool

Ordnance Survey Grid Reference SO 285006

OS Explorer Map 152

Derek says…

I've been to Pontypool many times over the years. In 2005, I had the great honour of switching on the Christmas lights. So being no stranger to the town, it was nice to come back and attempt this walk on a rainy Sunday.

It starts in the rolling splendour of Pontypool Park: a beautiful place where you can watch the rugby team in action or take part in many activities, such as bowls and tennis – not forgetting the dry ski slope.

Shell Grotto is probably the best preserved grotto in Wales. It's a steep hike up, but worth the effort. It doesn't look much from the outside, but once inside you're in for a real treat. The floor is made of the bones and teeth of animals, while the ceiling is covered with thousands of shells, minerals and real stalactites removed from local caves. Amazing!

From here it's up the hill to the Folly Tower and some of the best views in Torfaen. On a clear day, it is said you can see seven counties! If you have time, pop into the Valley Inheritance Museum where you can learn more about the proud history of the area.

This is a walk through time. After passing through park land from the Victorian and Regency periods, you walk with the Romans and Celtic saints on top of the hill, before returning once again to Victorian extravagance. You don't have to labour too long or hard to be rewarded with stunning views of distant hills, foreign lands (England!) and silvery waters.

People may not think of Pontypool as an ideal walking destination, but it is easily accessible by bus, car or train, and there are times you feel you have the whole mountainside to yourself. If you come in spring you will be drenched in cherry blossom, in the summer you can experience shady walks followed by hillside breezes, the autumn is ripe with sweet chestnuts and blackberries, while winter brings crisp, clean air and a steaming mug of hot chocolate at the end of your walk.

Fiona Ford

Torfaen Borough Counci

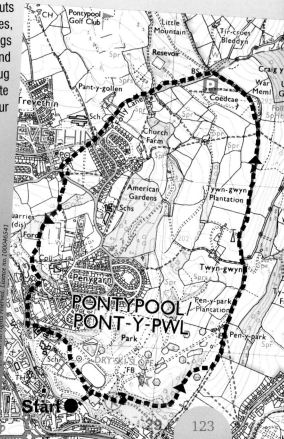

So far in this book we've stressed how much great walking can be found on your doorstep – or to put it another way – you don't have to head for the honeypot sites and famous names to get a great walk.

Take Pontypool for instance. Lovely as it is, it would not come high on a list of places to go walking and I doubt even if many of the people in the town itself know about some of the great trails and treats that lie in wait for them, just a mile outside the more urban post codes. On a crisp winter's morning though, a walk across the hills above the town offers some great views and lots of interesting places to explore.

The route we chose kicks off near the iconic home of the fabled Pontypool Front Row. Now we all know that Pontypool Park can draw a crowd on a match day but really rugby is just one of the attractions on offer here. Sports ground aside, the park runs to about 160 acres and boasts a museum and a selection of follies. The walk also takes in an historic church and a Roman road with a high-rise view of much of Gwent (and even the Severn crossing beyond).

This is a walk that is, once again, really easy to find as it starts in the car park near the town's leisure centre. Crossing over the small footbridge across the Afon Llwyd – a very grey river that used to be called the Torfaen (or 'rock breaker') – you pass the swimming pool, playground and café before you pull away to your right (with the rugby ground just on the hill above you to your left).

From here you stroll through the tree-lined park space before heading up the hill to your left on a partly-stepped trail that takes you into the trees. From here it becomes a short but fairly steep climb to the day's first folly. It's the first of three (and truthfully it's the least spectacular one too) and the slow pull up towards it gives you some great views of Pontymoile – once the home of young Reg Jones, who was brought up in the village by an aunt.

Reg who? Well you may know him as the Hollywood actor Ray Milland (there must have been another Reg Jones in Tinseltown, hence the change of name!).

The folly is a small gazebo, an arched stone alcove with a seat inside that makes for a good place to sit and catch your breath. It used to reside much further up the mountain and lay undiscovered for many years at the bottom of the garden of a house in Trevethin. Abandoned and overgrown, it had been wrongly identified as an old pigsty before someone realised exactly what it was – one of a group of follies built in the estate by the original owners, the Hanbury family.

The Hanburys came to Pontypool in the 1500s attracted by the town's reputation as a hub of the early iron-making industry. They bought an iron works (which now lies buried under the park grounds) and moved to the area, developing an estate which they later donated to the local authority as a public park. The little gazebo was carefully uncovered, taken apart and then moved stone by stone and rebuilt in its present position back in 2004. It's a natural sun-trap and from here you can see Sebastapol and Griffithstown, as well as the start of Cwmbran, while the mountain directly opposite is Mynydd Maen, easily identified by the aerial mast at the top (and the tracks down the side of it made by illegal motor bike scramblers).

From here it's another ten minutes of steady uphill walking until you reach the second folly – the Grotto. On the way there's more ammunition for the argument that you don't have to head for Snowdonia to get some great views.

As the slope begins to flatten you'll be treated to the gorgeous spread of much of the greener parts of Gwent, which falls away below you to your right (including Llandegfedd reservoir and the golf course at Green Meadow). Meanwhile behind you, the Transporter Bridge at Newport should be easy enough to pick out, and on a good day, you'll see both Severn bridge crossings.

Just ahead of you lies another little treat, hidden under a witch's hat of a roof. It's a squat round building that sits resolutely against the strong winds that gust over the crest of the hill here (and to see how strong – and regular – these are, take a look at the shapes of the surrounding tree tops).

This is the Grotto and the great shame is that this magical little place is only open sporadically throughout the year. It used to be left open at all times until vandals went inside and set fire to it. It was rebuilt and its interior lovingly restored in 1996 but no one would risk losing this unique building again – hence the locked gates and railings that encircle it today. If you want to see inside, check with the local council or leisure centre, who should be able to tell you which days it's open to the public (Torfaen even run 'Landrover safari's' up here for those who can't manage the walk and want to have a look around).

If you do get inside you'll be confronted by a bizarre piece of interior design, commissioned by Molly Hanbury Leigh in the early 1800s (at the height of a fashionable rage for grottos and follies). The grotto building was put up a little while before that in the late 1780s and it doubled as a hunting lodge for the family and their guests. Back then, the grotto stood in a deer park and the teeth and bones of some of the animals shot by the hunts now decorate the floor of the hut. Tear your eyes away from the macabre patterns of spinal column and teeth and look upwards and you'll see a fan-vaulted ceiling covered in sea shells, all picking out various geometrical patterns.

Real stalactites were taken from local caves and cemented into the walls too and were often topped off with pink conch shells for added effect. In 1882 the then Prince of Wales visited the grotto and had lunch here. Apparently he did complain that the champagne he had was corked, which of course, must have been a minor tragedy for him!

Leaving here we then head for the third and final folly, taking as our route an ancient track that meanders past old farmhouses and up onto the bare-headed moor of the mountain proper. There's little chance to get lost here because our destination is clearly visible throughout this section of the walk. It's an octagonal tower, about three stories high and topped with a turret effect.

Like the grotto it was built in the 1780s and was probably a summer house for the Hanbury family, although with its dominant position and unparalleled views it was also a decent place to spot game for the many hunting parties.

In fact its command of the landscape was so strong that during the Second World War it was demolished, for fear that German warplanes would use it as a reference point to spot the potential target of the nearby Glascoed bomb factory. The story didn't end there though as the tower was a well-loved landmark for the local population, who campaigned for years to get it re-built. They got their wish in the early 1990s when it was the turn of the current Prince of Wales to come to the old estate and officially re-open the old folly.

The tower is still accessible but like the grotto, it's permanently locked to discourage vandals and, again, is only open on rare occasions. There is a legend that it was built on the site of an old Roman fort or watch tower but there is little to back that myth up, aside from the fact that a Roman road runs within 100 yards of it.

That would make for a pretty good walk itself, running as it does from Mamhilad to Trevethin, into the valley over Pontnewenydd Bridge and back up the hill before reaching Llanhilleth Church. As it is we follow it past the cows and sheep of the farms at the top of the hill and down into the hamlet of Trevethin, nowadays a sadly run down estate which has little to tempt a walker into stopping. Its name comes from 'Trev Ithan which translates as 'town of gorse' and had you visited the area before the estate was built

that's pretty much what you would have seen – a hillside of scrub and gorse (and in fact much of the land above Tevethin resembles that today).

At the bottom of the hill lies the church of St Cadoc's, named after a man so holy that as an infant he climbed into the font three times during his baptism, much to the wonder and excitement of all who saw it as they recognised the act as a sign of his commitment to the holy Trinity.

Cadoc was a locally born saint who dates back to the 6th century and it was he who established the first church to stand on this spot, although legend has it that he had trouble building it. The story goes that every day Cadoc returned to the site, he would find the walls he had made the previous day knocked down and the stones scattered all around. Every day he would rebuild them only to return the following morning to a scene of damage and demolition. Unlike today, when such a strange set of events may be put down to 'some kids messing about', Cadoc found that he faced a much sterner challenge to his ambitions then a bunch of ASBO'd 'hoodies'. The reason his church was regularly demolished was, of course, the Devil, who stole into the grounds each night and destroyed Cadoc's hard work.

Handily for all concerned though, Cadoc had been given a miraculous bell by St Gilda, a bell which when rung, emitted a piercing, startling sound. Thus armed, Cadoc crept up on the dark lord, rang the bell and shocked the Devil into dropping the stones he was carrying and running away. Those stones, dropped by the vandalising demon, can be seen on the top of Mynydd Garnclochdy (although archaeologists might try and tell you that they belong to a Bronze Age cairn instead!). Subsequent attempts to re-build and expand the church did not meet with any further problems (of the supernatural or indeed of any other kind) and the current building belongs to the Victorian period, having been extensively remodelled in 1846.

All that remains of any earlier buildings is the main tower which dates back to the 13th century. It's a beautiful church with a gorgeous wooden Lych Gate entrance and an interesting graveyard. If you have the time to

wander through it, look out for the tiny iron crosses that mark the graves of some of the unfortunate men killed in one of the area's worst mining disasters.

In 1890, 176 men died in an explosion at the Llanerch Colliery, over the valley. What made the tragedy worse for the families of the victims was that most of the men had only been moved to the pit after they survived a fire in the nearby Glyn Pits which claimed the lives of five men. Having survived that terrifying underground blaze they were then killed in an even bigger disaster. There is a memorial stained glass window to the men inside the church. Another grave of note is that of Private John Jobbins, a survivor of the battle at Rorke's Drift, who was buried here with full military honours in 1934.

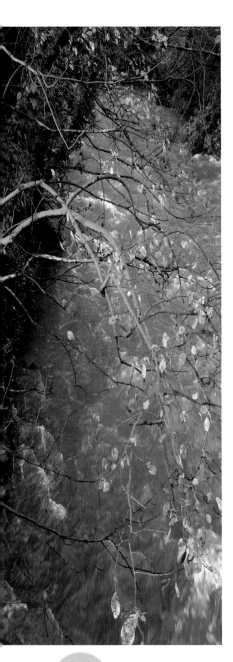

Leaving the church you cross the main road and walk through a gate at the side of the Yew Tree pub. A former landlord of this pub, John Summerfield, was once the fattest man in England and when he was not touring in exhibitions around the country, people would come from miles around to gawp at his 67 inch waist. He died in 1855, aged just 34 but weighing in at a whopping 34 stone. Before his funeral, the undertaker had to wait while Summerfield's bedroom window was removed so that the body could be taken out of the house and carried across the road to the cemetery opposite.

From here you follow a gravel path downhill, which used to be known as the 'cobbled walk'. It was a path specially built by the Hanbury family to let their servants walk to church, through the woods and fields of the estate, without getting mud on their clothes and spoiling their Sunday Best. It has recently been upgraded, the cobbled edges being retained and an all-weather surface replacing the main path to allow access for everyone.

That path will then take you back down into Pontypool. As you make your way back down to the leisure centre there's still plenty of evidence of the old estate to pass on the way. The first thing you'll come across are the old ice houses. Recently refurbished, they are unique because of their unusual 'double chambered' design.

Another relic of the family's tenure (which you can stop off and visit on your walk home) is the old Georgian stable block which now houses the town's museum. Inside it is a collection of 'Japanware'. Japanning was a method of decorative lacquering applied to all kinds of products and pioneered at Pontypool during the Industrial Revolution. In fact, legend has it that Charles Hanbury gave Catherine the Great of Russia a number of Japanware products made at Pontypool when he was ambassador to her court in 1757. The name comes from the Japanese lacquered goods that were being imported into Britain at that time and which this process attempted to mimic.

The Hanbury foundry at Pontypool had also devised a way of rolling out thin tin plate which was adapted to make lacquered snuff boxes and other luxury items (which sold for relatively high prices across the country).

The museum also houses a section detailing the life of a Victorian domestic servant, which given its proximity to that old cobbled path is quite apt. From the museum it's then a straightforward walk back to the car park and the start point – a satisfying circular route that should give you a new perspective of this old Welsh town. As such it's also a walk of contrasts.

There is an obvious clash between the Pontypool of the Hanbury's hey day – a town of industrial innovation, harnessed to the drive and ambition of the times while financing the high life of the family itself – and the sleepy rustic hamlet that existed before the 'Age of Manufactures'. There's also an obvious contrast with the town as it stands today.

But this is a walk that allows you to strip away the 21st century and get a glimpse into the town's past – a past which was both pastoral and violent, prosperous and exploitative. Above all it gives you a clear picture of how one powerful family can leave its mark on a landscape and a people. And as you kick off your walking boots back at the car park, you might realise that having 'stepped through the ages', you're unlikely to look at the town in the same way again.

Llanwonno

Near: Rhondda

Ordnance Survey Grid Reference ST 031015

OS Explorer Map 166

This walk is a real gem, showing you a more peaceful side to the Rhondda Valley. Everyone I met was down to earth and friendly. It takes you through some beautiful countryside which has one of the largest forests in Wales, a rediscovered well, a picturesque waterfall and the Clydach Reservoir.

The walk starts in the remote village of Llanwynno where Ferndale Male Voice Choir sang 'Men of Harlech' for the film *Zulu*. Have a look inside St Gwynno's church which dates back to the 6th century – it's so quiet you can hear your heart beat! The famous runner, Guto Nyth Bran, is buried here.

Stop for a picnic at Pistyll Goleu but watch out for midges! This 26-foot waterfall used to be a Victorian tourist attraction.

Llanwynno Forest is a haven of birdlife; at night the area attracts twitchers in their droves, seeking the nightjar. By day, you can spot woodcock and other species. And it's definitely worth climbing up 'Old Smokey'. The views are stunning: on a clear day you can see the Brecon Beacons, Cardiff and the Bristol Channel. Finally, finish off with a drink or Sunday lunch in the popular Brynffynnon pub.

This is an easy walk of about four miles, with an optional steep climb for the more energetic. Llanwonno Forest is tucked away between the Rhondda and Aberdare valleys, a hidden rural area with a rich history, lying just north of the village of Ynysybwl.

Spend time exploring Saint Gwynno's Church, look for the grave of Guto Nyth Bran and visit the site of Gwynno's Well – the waters are reputed to have healing powers!

The route through the peaceful forest area leads to the hidden Clydach Reservoir, built in the Victorian era. You can then take a detour to climb to the top of Tylorstown Tip – a legacy of the Rhondda Valley coal industry – from which you will get views over the Vale of Glamorgan and up into the Brecon Beacons.

Kevin Oates

Rhondda Countryside Ranger

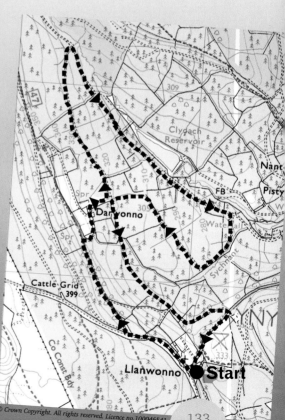

133

CAUGHT between the Cynon and Rhondda valleys – two big centres of population – this spot should be teeming with walkers. But just like Pontypool, here's another example of how much great, gorgeous 'walkable' countryside is sat on people's doorsteps, crying out for some Welsh feet to wander all over. Llanwonno is yet another little gem of a ramble that should attract more visitors. Trust us, it may be short and easy to do (and there's nothing wrong with that!) but it has a lot to offer willing walkers.

It has a lot to offer drivers too. The car journey from the Rhondda side, above Ferndale and Blaenllecheu, is a spectacular crawl above the valley towns sprawled below. The twists and turns of the hill topography below you makes for a dizzying, vertical drive, while the single lane track, shadowed by a broken dry stone wall, will induce a momentary bout of vertigo in most travellers.

It's also a punishing stretch of road much loved by masochistic mountain bikers, but for those who prefer to use two walking-boot-clad feet, the real treats start once you hit the top of the mountain and approach St Gwynno's Forest.

This walk takes you through the forest and kicks off in the car park below the hamlet of Llanwonno. It's made up of one pub (the Bryn Ffynnon Arms) and one church. And nothing else. Now how Welsh is that?

Walking from the car park towards the Bryn Ffynnon Arms, you hit the top of a small hill and look down and across to the pub and St Gwynno's. The first thing you notice is the sheer size of the churchyard. It seems totally out of proportion for such a small place. But the ancient parish of Llanwynno also included Abercynon, Ynysybwl, parts of Mountain Ash and Pontypridd as well as Porth, Wattstown and Blaenllechau.

It's a graveyard that can also boast a genuine Welsh folk hero too. St Gwynno's is the final resting place of the legendary runner Guto Nyth Bran. Born in 1700 in the village of Llwyncelyn (Hollybush) in the Rhondda, he moved with his family to the farm of Nyth Bran (hence the nickname) while a baby. It was as a young man, working with his father rounding up sheep on the mountains, that his remarkable speed and endurance came to people's notice. He once caught a bird in full flight and chased down a hare on a hillside, but it was running an errand for his mother that set him on course for fame and fortune. She sent him to a shop in Pontypridd to pick up some food, a round trip of seven miles. Guto did it in the time it took his mother to boil the breakfast kettle – or so they say (keep in mind that this was no fancy electric kettle and that this time has never been independently verified!).

Anyway, Sian o'r Siop, who ran the little store, was quick to realise the potential in this remarkable speed merchant and so she took him under her wing, training the young man and managing his racing career. She also became his sweetheart and soon arranged a race with an army captain stationed in Carmarthen. Guto beat the more experienced man over a four mile course in Hirwaun and pocketed £400 in prize money.

It didn't take long for Guto to run out of worthy opponents and the unbeatable athlete soon retired to domestic bliss.

Many years later, however, a new champion named Prince appeared on the scene and Sian encouraged her husband to train again and take him on. With a thousand guineas at stake the two men were set to run over a 12-mile course from St Woolo's church in Newport to St Barrwg's in Bedwas.

Despite being behind for much of the race, Guto came through on the final uphill climb to beat the younger man, finishing in a time of 53 minutes. Sian was the first to congratulate him, excitedly slapping him on the back. As she did so her husband fell to the ground. He died in her arms and was carried away by grieving supporters to the church of St Gwynno's.

The original gravestone, marked with a simple heart (to symbolise his love for Sian) now lies over the grave, while a later headstone bears an inscription in Welsh (there is a translation on a small plaque by the corner of the church).

His grave is one of many jumbled around the entrance to the church, with the oldest dating back to 1667. The twisted ancient yew trees in the cemetery also hint at older pagan worship and the church also contains a relic stone dating back to the 9th century.

Opposite the church is a signpost with a bike sign and a red number 47 written on it. This refers to the long-distance cycle path that shares this part of the walk. Route 47 is a high level ride that runs from Pontypridd down to Neath – a stunning cycle track that clocks in at around 22 miles, mostly through forestry.

Walkers follow the main road here, going past the church for a few hundred yards and then turning right onto a bridleway at a sign marked Daerwynno. You are now in a beech-filled wood that slowly turns into conifer forest, walking on a wide private road that's straight and flat and easy to follow.

It leads to the Daerwynno Centre, a bunkhouse and outdoor pursuits hall, based at the old farm of St Gwynno's.

Run by local volunteers (the Cwm Clydach Outdoor Activity Group) the centre runs outdoor activities and educational courses from canoeing and climbing to team building and wildlife studies.

You cut through the old farm and leave by a kissing gate at the bottom of the compound, to join up with a signposted Loops and Link Walk, a dedicated network of paths looked after by the local Rhondda Cynon Taff Council.

From here you start to go deeper into the forest. It's become a popular destination for bird watchers over the years with the main attraction being a resident population of nightjars. 'Twitchers' have been known to meet in the local Brynffynon pub and then wait until darkness when the birds are active (they tend to favour the recently felled parts of the forest where the ground more closely resembles the heath and moorland where they are more usually found).

If you fancy an atmospheric bout of bird watching here in the late evenings then be warned – the gnats will eat you alive! During the day though, you could be rewarded with sightings of chaffinches, crossbills, goldcrests, kestrels and even the odd woodcock or goshawk.

The forest also boasts pine martens, polecats, foxes and badgers as well as smooth and palmate newts.

The paths are all bordered by drainage ditches and various streams and in spring they are all

full of frogs and frog spawn. Walk here at that time of year and you'll see (and hear them) splashing through the water as you wander through.

At a T-junction after half a mile or so, the path begins to turn right, allowing you to see the breadth of the valley as the pine forest starts to fall away in front of you.

Ignore the track descending to your left, and keep to the higher path which starts to reveal glimpses of a reservoir below. This is the Clydach Reservoir, built in the late 1800s to supply water to the then expanding pit communities of Ynysbwl and Glyn Coch.

With the local Lady Windsor colliery long gone, the reservoir is no longer used for water storage and its main function seems to be in providing the local Daerwynno Centre with a place for canoeing and raft-building. It's also a popular picnic spot and is never allowed to run dry, mainly because the dam here has a clay core and if it dried out it could collapse.

It's a beautiful, peaceful spot and a great place to rest up and take in the view, with the placid, mirror-glass surface of the water reflecting the winter colours of the countryside. Below it are the remains of an old railway line built to bring in stone for the reservoir from Ynysbwl. These days it's just another lost by-way of the industrial age, abandoned to nature and turned over to the walkers and wildlife. From the reservoir you follow the path and head for the Pistyll Goleu waterfall.

There are ankle-high markers all along the path here and the green arrows take you to a set of steps that lead down to the river bank and a viewing point looking up at the waterfall. It's no Sgud Eira but it's another pretty spot and was popular with Victorian walkers, although be warned that the wooden chicken-wire covered steps can be a bit slippery – so watch your step.

From here it's a straight walk out back to the main road and the car park where we started. But there is one more final site of interest that's worth making the effort to see.

There are two holy wells in the Rhondda. The first is high above the valley in Penrhys and is marked by a small shrine. The second is here in Llanwonno and lies just off the main road, in the dip below the churchyard. A small foot-high sign shows the way through a recently planted column of trees.

Follow the slight, twisting path and you are rewarded with what must be the least spectacular holy site you could wish to find: a small pond, about three feet across, fed by a spring, with what at first looks like a 'Keep off the Grass' sign stuck at the side. Actually it's a wooden marker saying 'St Gwynno's Holy Well'!

The water was supposed to have amazing restorative powers, but with the frogs swimming through it, the well isn't that tempting. Still, in its day, it was a big attraction and the view from the well to the

churchyard makes for a nice end to this easy circular walk.

In fact, the whole route is peaceful and calming, while the wander through the scented pine forest is a nice way to spend any day. It's the kind of undemanding, restful walk that warrants repeated visits, the attraction being in the wildlife and wildflowers, the sounds and the smells as much as in the views. And with a handy pub at the end of the path, a fascinating churchyard to mull over and the reservoir and waterfall to idle at, it packs a lot into its short distance.

Really, places like this shouldn't be so quiet but this is the reward of walking. And on a clean, crisp winter's day, you could do worse then wander through Llanwonno.

Bethlehem

Near: Llandeilo

Ordnance Survey Grid Reference SN 687263

OS Explorer Map OL12

Derek says...

C armarthenshire may be the gateway to Pembrokeshire, but you don't have to travel beyond the county boundary to go walking. Carmarthenshire has some of the finest walks in Wales, with a wonderful coastline, rolling countryside, castles, and hills rising to over 2,500 feet.

Our walk begins in Bethlehem, a hamlet perched on a hillside in a remote corner of the Brecon Beacons National Park. The walk, which joins the Beacons Way, is packed with history and superb views across the Towy Valley.

People from all over the world come to Bethlehem because of the biblical name, which derives from its chapel. This walk can be done at any time, but come in December and take your Christmas cards to the local post office to be stamped with the famous Bethlehem postmark.

One other tip. After our walk, Toby, our guide, took me for a slap-up Sunday roast at the Plough Inn in Myddfai – very tasty after a long winter walk!

This moderate walk of approximately four miles encompasses the beautiful area of Bethlehem in Carmarthenshire. It takes in some of the many historical and archaeological sites of the area, with spectacular views over the Towy valley.

Starting from the village, a short section of the Beacons Way will take you up to the ramparts of Garn Goch, the magnificent Iron Age hill fort which dominates the landscape. Here you will find a host of wildlife such as green woodpeckers feeding on anthills, adders basking amongst the rocks (beware!) and red kites soaring overhead. You will then pass through the ruins of a deserted hamlet cloaked in woodland and the site of an ancient Roman villa before returning by road to Bethlehem.

This walk is lovely in any season, but perfect on a crisp winter's day, when you can return to Llandeilo or Llangadog for warm food and drink, or as Derek did, enjoy a nice plate of mince pies!

Toby Small
Area Warden, Brecon Beacons National Park.

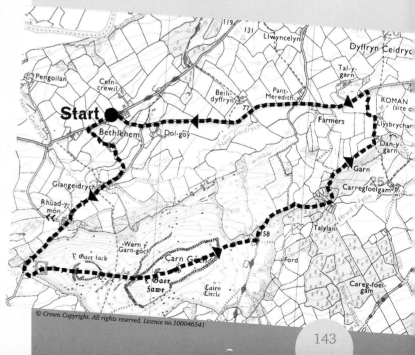

OK so you've almost got to the end of a year's worth of Welsh walks. And with December left there's really only one place to recommend – the little village of Bethlehem. You'll find it nestled just inside the western border of the Brecon Beacons National Park (making it the fourth walk in the Beacons for this book).

Bethlehem lies in the Tywi Valley (to the northeast of Llandeilo and the southwest of Llangadog) and is the end point of the Beacons Way, a 100-mile trail that traverses the Park, from east to west.

It's an eight-day walk – promoted as the path that links Bethlehem to the Holy Mountain, which is what some people call the Skirrid in

Abergavenny, the mountain that features at the start of the route. Our little ramble clocks in at a much more manageable three to four hours, depending on the weather, your fitness and your curiosity.

This just about registers as a village, as it's little more than a hamlet consisting of a scattered collection of homes, a primary school, a village hall, a post office and a Nonconformist chapel.

It's the latter two buildings that Bethlehem owes its reputation to. The village was originally called Dyffryn Ceidrich but was renamed Bethlehem in honour of the chapel, built in the 1800s during the Welsh Methodist Revival. The change in name eventually led to a seasonal investigation of the village by the curious and the festive-minded and from the 1960s onwards it became a tradition for people to get their Christmas cards franked in the town's post office. These are dispatched all over the globe from this one tiny little place (now where was the 'franking sense' in that?!).

Despite the regular December overload, however, the post office did close for a period of about 14 years back in 1988, during which time all the Bethlehem cards were redirected through Llandeilo. But while they were still franked as Bethlehem, it wasn't really the same thing, so in 2002 the post office was reopened (bucking a national trend) and as such the custom continues to this day. In 2007, for instance, around 30,000 letters and cards were posted from here, each bearing the angel and harp stamp with a bilingual Christmas greeting.

The rest of the village has not been slow in capitalising on the market value of the name either, and every year Bethlehem hosts a traditional Christmas market in the run up to the big day, drawing visitors from all over Wales.

The post office also doubles as a community hall, and is the place where our walk kicks off. From here you head through the village towards the chapel, which is halfway along an up-and-down hill with a wicked early incline. We walked past here on a chilly Sunday morning, just as the cars

carrying the congregation were starting to pull up outside. In no time, their hymn singing was sending us on our way as we began the slow climb up towards Garn Goch, a bare-headed mountain burned brown and red with winter bracken.

It may have been the singing, it may have been the hazy light and seasonal mist, but there is definitely a 'spiritual' atmosphere to this walk. Long before the Revivalists christened this place Bethlehem, the area had a reputation for holiness and in the 5th and 6th centuries it was famous for producing more homegrown saints than any other part of Wales. It also has that tangible sense of the past and of tradition, something that only comes when a place has been lived in over thousands of years. The evidence of that habitation lies ahead at the top of the mountain.

Before you get there, however, you pass an old stone enclosure (although in Beacons terms it's fairly recent, having sat on the hillside for no more than 200 years or so). The ruin is a former animal pen, a circular stone compound for stabling sheep or other grazing animals. You pass it on your left, near the top of the hill, before turning into a car park area at the foot of Garn Goch.

From here you head up a muddy path towards a large standing stone. This is Gwynfor's Stone, a large (seven feet high by about four feet across) rock which serves as a monument to the man who was Plaid Cymru's first MP, Gwynfor Evans. Evans was elected as the MP for Camarthen on July 14, 1966, in an historic by-election win. He died in April 2005, aged 92, and the stone, which is engraved with the emblem of Plaid Cymru, was erected in 2006, forty years after that victory.

From the stone you can admire the Tywi Valley in all its glory, with Llandeilo in the west, perched on the banks of the river. The view stretches all the way up to Llangadog in the east, and if the weather's with you, then you might catch a red kite hovering above the glorious landscape. Of course, if the weather's *not* with you, then you might get to see the Tywi in full flood instead – which to be fair, from this height, is equally spectacular.

The main drag from here to Garn Goch can be busy, but it's a

comfortable up-and-down ramble of a route on which walkers are usually accompanied by a raven or two swooping overhead, whatever the time of year. If you walk this way in the summer months then remember to watch where you're stepping, as the bracken can prove to be a playground for snakes (adders, in actual fact). Lazy serpents are prone to sunbathe on southern slopes before the sun warms them up and in this state they can be quite sluggish. As such there's less chance of them getting out of the way before you see them – so be careful.

Meanwhile, birdwatchers are advised to watch the lumps and bumps of the anthill mounds that bubble and burst over the bare patches of land here. The reason? Well sometimes – if you're lucky – you might catch a green woodpecker perched on one, rooting around inside for a quick snack.

No chance of that happening on a December walk though, so instead keep your eyes peeled for the piles of stones that mark the lower entrance to the old hill fort. Garn Goch (or the Red Cairn) is one of the largest Iron and Bronze Age settlements in Wales, and it commands the landscape from this dominant position (it tops the hill at around 700 feet above sea

level). Marked out by some massive stone defences (which tower above you as you walk up to the top of the hill) the whole site runs to around 28 acres. As such, it's a fantastic place to explore. It gets its name from the large stone cairn at the middle of the settlement. Meanwhile the reference to 'red' either comes from the russet glow that the sun casts on the bracken or from the blood spilled in the countless battles that raged around these hills over 2,000 years ago.

To call it a fort is somewhat misleading as this was not a garrison, but a fortified community featuring animal enclosures and a number of dwellings. A lot of Iron Age forts were based around extended family groups, but the remains here are on a scale that suggests a level of resources, manpower and political significance way beyond that provided by such a small arrangement of people. Make no mistake, this was an important place and at the height of its power it would have been without equal in prehistoric Wales.

The construction of Garn Goch follows the contours of the hill itself, making it particularly secure and well defended. Although nowadays it's no more than a mass of weathered stone, as you roam around its ramparts, you still get a sense of its strength and significance. The ruins here break down into two distinct sets of defences called Y Gaer Fach (the small fort) and Y Gaer Fawr (the large fort). No prizes for guessing why. They are placed on two separate summits on the same long ridge, with Y Gaer Fach the more run-down of the two.

Wherever you wander here, though, you will be struck by the eeriness of the place. This is a long-lost Celtic community which, thousands of years ago, would have teemed with life. Catch it on a cold misty December morning, and the ghosts and echoes of that time seem to hang in the air, part of the mist that clings to the craggy rocks and broken battlements. Definitely a place to make your imagination cartwheel and the hairs on the back of your neck stand up.

After exploring the ruins, head down the other side of the hill towards the back road that runs behind it. Turn left onto the road and make for a cattle grid, where you should spot another significant stone construction – although this time on a much smaller scale! On your right hand side you should see a little rock figure made from a handful of large wall stones. This is an inukshuk, a small statue, made by a visiting Dutch sculptor who specialises in Arctic and Northern Scandinavian native art. An inukshuk (which is Innuit for 'looks like a man') is a small stone statue used

by tribes to mark the way to the good hunting grounds and fishing holes. They are supposed to show how an inhospitable landscape can support human habitation (so I try not to ponder too long on the significance of finding one in Carmarthenshire!). Still it's another curiosity that makes the walk more interesting and it points us in the direction of the home leg of the journey, through two more historical periods.

Before you make it to the first, however, the landscape changes, and you enter a pine forest, which borders more traditional Welsh woodland. Keep your eyes peeled and you may spot some strange stockade-style fencing, a criss-cross collection of thick, sharpened logs, ringing the trunks of some of the trees. These are part of a mushroom farm, with the fungi grown on the sides of the logs in a traditional Japanese method of cultivation. Grown in this way, the mushrooms are easy to pick and less likely to get infected with algae or moss.

Just down the path from the fungi farm comes another walkers' treat – a long lost village, abandoned back in the 1920s. Called Pentre Bach, it was a classic Welsh rural hamlet, a scattered collection of cottages which were given up, one by one, as the villagers moved down into Bethlehem. The last house was vacated in the 1930s and over the years, the slate and stone has been removed, allowing the elements to gently unpick the structures.

The walk takes you past a few of these old cottages and they are all worth a brief look. You'll find them stood in the middle of overgrown orchards and old enclosures (now overrun by the forest) and many of the dilapidated dwellings still have their old hearths and fire places intact. One has a 60-year-old ash tree growing out of what used to be a living room.

The ruins of Pentre Bach lead you back even further in time as the walk winds its way towards Llys Brychan. This was the name of an old Roman villa that once stood here, although there's nothing to see at the site today.

To those of us who wander by, it's just an unploughed field, but a series of archaeological digs have turned up various bits of Roman flotsam and jetsam (mostly tiles and pottery) and the quality of the finds suggests that this was a house owned by an important and wealthy man. In all probability, it belonged to a local chieftain who had 'gone Roman'.

What tended to happen, after the initial period of invasion and contested early occupation, was that the foreign forces would begin to 'bed in' with the local population. The two would begin to trade, and slowly the locals would start to work with the Romans, before finally adopting their style and tastes. So the villa is a perfect example of how the Welsh got on with life under the Roman Empire and gave up opposing it. It's a nice contrast to the Celtic remains on the hillside above, which would still have retained their impressive power and threat on the horizon while the Romans, garrisoned at Llandeilo, got on with their business on the land below.

It's also a nice way to finish the walk, as it was the Romans, of course, who created Christmas in the first place. They took their ancient festival of Saturnalia and sanitised it by declaring 25 December the birth date of Christ. Thus the merriment, lights, gifts and decoration of Saturnalia were successfully allied to the spiritual demands of the Christian celebration. Something to think about, maybe, as you head back down towards Bethlehem, as the drag and the pull of Christmas shopping and family dinners will no doubt begin to creep back into your mind with the walk nearly done.

Last Orders

OK, so by now you've wandered (mentally at least) through 12 months of recommended Welsh walks. But maybe you're still looking for a little extra encouragement to finally get you out of your house and into the great outdoors?

Well, how about some company on the walk, or your own expert or guide to help you? Better still, what about a few dates for your diary, just to help focus the mind. Would that work? OK, no problem, we can do that for you. You see, Wales is finally waking up to the possibilities of walking tourism, and slowly but surely, we are putting together a package of events, resources, accommodation and expertise to capitalise on our potential for foot-powered fun.

At the forefront of this drive to get more people walking in Wales is the growth in walking festivals. These can offer the best entry point for exploring the countryside.

In the first *Weatherman Walking* book, we ended by listing the various National Parks associations, walking associations and County Councils best placed to point you in the direction of a good route and good advice.

1. Barmouth Walking Festival

Barmouth is a small but beautiful seaside town with a distinct Victorian stamp, nestled below Dinas Oleu (the fortress of light) – the first land owned by the National Trust. Surrounded by the splendour of the Snowdonia National Park, it also has the good fortune to enjoy the backdrop of the Rhinog Mountains to the north east, Cader Idris to the south east, and to the north, gorgeous views of the Llŷn Peninsula. The festival runs in late September, and in 2008 it boasted 25 guided walks including Dollgellau to Aberllefenni, Maentwrog to the Vale of Ffestiniog, and a great route from Beddgelert to Moel Hebog.

If you've never visited this part of the country before, then this is a fantastic way to get acquainted with some stunning walks. And as far as festivals goes, this is one of the best (in fact it was nominated for a top Wales National Tourism award in 2007).

2. Anglesey Walking Festival

Held in late June (and already name-checked once in this book) this is probably the biggest festival in Wales featuring a mammoth 52 guided walks as well as a special five-day programme for primary schoolchildren (aimed at years 5 and 6). Walks have included bird-watching expeditions, bat-watching evenings and routes themed around the bridges of Menai, the industry around Parys Copper Mountain and the port at Amlwch.

You could also use it to copy our very own Newborough and Llanddwyn walk (see chapter three) and if coastal walks are your thing, you'll be hard pressed to beat the Seven Beaches path, based around the island's north east coast.

3. Wales Valleys Walking Festival

This is a bit of an odd one in that it's a collection of walks spread out over a wide area with no real centre to promote the event. Having said that, it's a great introduction to some often neglected (or maybe just overlooked) walking country – like Blaenau Gwent and the Rhondda. Also, these walks cover a host of towns with big populations (well, in Welsh terms anyway!), including places like Merthyr Tydfil, Ebbw Vale and Caerphilly. So this festival is a great opportunity for people to get out and enjoy the good things on their doorstep.

This is another late September event and one other bonus, is that the programme of walks (there are around 25 different events) is divided into easy-to-follow levels of required effort.

Easy Walks include a Rhydyfelin River Walk and an amble around the lake at Bryn Bach Park, Tredegar, while more challenging routes include the Hendre Mynydd Hop in Rhondda, and a circuit walk along the ridges surrounding Pontypridd.

4. Prestatyn Walking Festival

Held in early May, this is a festival that can boast some big routes like the Offa's Dyke National Trail, the North Wales Path, and some great walks in the Clwydian and Dee ranges.

It's also a festival which likes to have a theme – so, for example, in 2008, the walks were collected under the banner of 'the Romans in North East Wales'. As such, visitors were treated to history trails like 'the Lost Roman City of Varae' and 'A Saint, a Goblin Stone and a Sacred Hill'. There was also one called 'A 007 Adventure Walk', which may have bent the Roman guidelines somewhat but at least gives you a flavour of what a wide and fun programme of events this is.

5. Crickhowell Walking Festival

Crickhowell is a pretty market town in the Brecon Beacons, a few miles west of Abergavenny and an hour from the Severn Bridge. The great thing about this festival is that it's held in early March (the last one started on 1 March, St David's Day) so if you've had this book for Christmas then it's the ideal event to get you started!

In 2008 the festival ran 38 walks packed with real diversity. There were Welsh learners' walks, a poetry walk, an artists' walk and a town treasure hunt too, while there were also a number of walks for children (aged 6 to 16). Other more traditional highlights included a walk up Table Mountain (obviously not the South African one!) and two walks which we featured in the first *Weatherman Walking* book – Llanthony Priory, in the Black Mountains and a walk around Mynydd Llangorse.

6. Cardigan Walking Festival

All the walks in this programme have traditionally been free and start within ten miles of Cardigan (with transport arranged to and from the start and finish points). It's a festival with a good variety of walks which explore the likes of the Teifi Valley (with Cilgerran Gorge and Cenarth falls), the area's coastal paths, the Preselis and the hinterland around Cardigan. As one of the later festivals (it usually starts in early October) it also means it can prolong your walking holiday season and give you a real taste of autumn walking.

7. Conwy Walking Week

Held in July, this is another event that boasts a varied and interesting programme. There are 34 walks on offer here, as always ranked in terms of length and ability, and they cover a wide stretch of enjoyable walking country, from the Great Orme to Pentrefoelas, Llanfairfechan to Abergele and the Ogwen Valley to Llansannan.

The programme has boasted the likes of a history walk based on the mountain men of Pen, another on the role the Orme played in World War Two and a folk tales walk centred on the area around Pentrefoelas and Ysbyty Ifan. Expect more of the same when you bring your boots to town.

8. Denbighshire Walking Weekend

Short and sweet, this is a long weekend of guided walks in Hiraethog and the Vale of Clwyd, held in late September. There is a three-day long, 32-mile challenge of a walk, which runs from Denbigh through to Llanrhaedr and Clocaenog before ending at Llyn Brenig.

If that's a bit too hardcore for your tastes then there is also a selection of easier routes, and in the past these have included things like a special 'step-back-in-time walk' where an archeologist will guide you around the Iron Age hill fort at Penycloddiau. So it's a chance for a spot of mental exercise as well as a physical work-out (the perfect kind of *Weatherman Walking* route in actual fact!).

9. Gower Walking Festival

Held over most of June, this is another 'big daddy' of the Welsh walking festival season. As you'll no doubt be familiar from the earlier chapter in this book, Gower is a walkers' paradise, with over 332 km (or 200 miles in old money) of public footpaths criss-crossing this little piece of heaven on Earth.

The festival comprises around 30 guided walks which range in distance from two to 18 miles in length. Like the majority of festivals, there are walks to suit all abilities (including a wheelchair route or two, and walks to accommodate prams and push chairs), while the trails offered in the past have also drawn heavily on the Rhossili journey showcased in this book.

10. Heart of Wales Walking Festival

Last but not least, this is yet another September event (well, I guess it does extend the tourist season past the summer holidays) based around the town of Llandrindod Wells. This event has a choice of some all-day walks (with scheduled stops for pub lunches) as well as half-day routes and shorter strolls for the less able (or – in the case of the kids walking – the easily bored).

In the past, the festival has also boasted a good programme of themed walks, like church walks, natural history walks and geology walks, while families have been catered for with events like a town architecture walk.

Of course, you don't have to wait for a festival to visit any of these places, but if you're an inexperienced walker or you just like some company and an informative guide on your walk, then these kinds of events are a godsend. Obviously we've listed the months that these traditionally take place, but as the majority are still in the planning phase as regards their next festival programme, if you're interested in finding out more, then Google the relevant event, contact the organisers, and keep yourself abreast of developments.

One final thought. If, while reading through this list of recommended Welsh walking centres, you found yourself scratching your head and reaching for the road atlas at the mention of certain names, then maybe we've highlighted just how much of the country still awaits your discovery. Wales is blessed with so much awe-inspiring beauty and so many magical places. It hoards stories and legends in the every corner, nook and cranny. We have an embarrassment of riches here and there's no better way to unearth them than by walking and unlocking this treasure with your own two feet. This is your country. Go enjoy it.

Discover the fun of walking in Wales with twelve more of über-weatherman Derek Brockway's favourite Welsh routes.

Hot on the heels of the best-selling *Weatherman Walking*, Derek is offering you another chance to walk in his footsteps and enjoy exactly the same exhilerating experience as portrayed on his popular BBC Wales TV show.

He has compiled another volume of gems based on his radio and television travels and arranged them over twelve months for a full year's worth of fantastic walks.

Written with series producer Julian Carey, *More Weatherman Walks* includes maps, directions and an insight into the social history, heritage, wildlife and topography of some of Wales's most attractive landscapes as well as including extra stories and secrets not revealed in the television series.

If you want to explore Wales on foot or from your armchair then Derek makes the ideal guide and companion.

Derek was born in Barry, South Wales and has been passionately interested in the weather ever since he was a young boy. A qualified meteorologist, he has been employed by the Met Office for over 20 years and became the main weather forecaster for BBC Wales in 1997. He now presents a number of radio and television programmes, including *Derek's Welsh Weather* and *Weatherman Walking*. His autobiography, *Whatever the Weather*, was published in 2007, and his leisure activities include walking, squash, skiing and learning Welsh.

BBC Wales

ISBN 978-1-84771-058-1

y Lolfa

photographs: Julian Car
design: Y Lolfa
www.ylolfa.com

£8.95

9 781847 710581

What's in the Egg?

Collins **Big Cat**

Moira Butterfield

Collins
Big Cat

Published by Collins
An imprint of HarperCollins*Publishers*
77–85 Fulham Palace Road
Hammersmith
London
W6 8JB

Browse the complete Collins catalogue at
www.collinseducation.com

Author: Moira Butterfield
Series editor: Cliff Moon

10 9 8 7 6 5 4 3 2 1

ISBN 978-0-00-751260-7

British Library Cataloguing in Publication Data
A catalogue record for this publication is available from the British Library.

Designer: Dan Newman, Perfect Bound Ltd
Design manager: Nikki Kenwood
Picture researcher: Frances Vargo
Reading ideas author: Clare Dowdall

Acknowledgements
Photographs: Front cover: Alamy/WILDLIFE GmbH; back cover: Getty Images/National Geographic Society/Jason Edwards; p1: Photoshot/NHPA/Laurie Campbell; p2, left: Corbis/Alaska Stock; p2, right: Getty Images/Discovery Channel Images/Jeff Foott; p3: Getty Images/Japan Images/Tohoku Color Agency; p3, inset: Corbis/Morten Andersen; p4, left: Alamy/mauritius images GmbH; p4, right: Getty Images/National Geographic Society/Jason Edwards; p5, right: naturepl.com/Luiz Claudio Marigo; p6, left: SuperStock/Animals Animals; p6, right: Photoshot/NHPA/Andre Baertschi; p7, right: naturepl.com/Simon Williams; p8, left: Photoshot/NHPA/Laurie Campbell; p8, right: Alamy/WILDLIFE GmbH; p9, right: naturepl.com/Philippe Clement; p10, left: naturepl.com/Tony Phelps; p10, right: Alamy/David Boag; p11, right: Getty Images/Peter Arnold/James Gerholdt; p12, left: Getty Images/Discovery Channel Images/Jeff Foott; p12, right: Alamy/Alaska Stock; p13, right: Photoshot/Juniors Tierbildarchiv.

Collins would like to thank the teachers and children at the following schools who took part in the development of Collins Big Cat:

John Betts Primary School
Redgate Primary School
Somerville Primary School
Springcroft Primary School
St James' C of E (C) Primary School
St Paul's C of E Primary School
The Crescent Primary School
Bilingual English Slovak School Trnava (BESST)
St Paul's British Primary School Brussels

Printed and bound by Printing Express Limited, Hong Kong

Get the latest Collins Big Cat news at
www.collinsbigcat.com

MIX
Paper from
responsible sources
FSC
www.fsc.org   FSC™ C007454

What's in the Egg?

Written by Moira Butterfield

Collins